Getting Started with Containers in Azure

Deploy Secure Cloud Applications Using Terraform

Second Edition

Shimon Ifrah

Getting Started with Containers in Azure: Deploy Secure Cloud Applications
Using Terraform

Shimon Ifrah
Melbourne, VIC, Australia

ISBN-13 (pbk): 978-1-4842-9971-5   ISBN-13 (electronic): 978-1-4842-9972-2
https://doi.org/10.1007/978-1-4842-9972-2

Managing Director, Apress Media LLC: Welmoed Spahr
Acquisitions Editor: Smriti Srivastava
Development Editor: Laura Berendson
Copy Editor: Jana Weinstein
Editorial Project Manager: Shaul Elson

Cover designed by eStudioCalamar

Cover image by Bolivia Inteligente on Unsplash (www.unsplash.com)

Distributed to the book trade worldwide by Apress Media, LLC, 1 New York Plaza, New York, NY 10004, U.S.A. Phone 1-800-SPRINGER, fax (201) 348-4505, e-mail orders-ny@springer-sbm.com, or visit www.springeronline.com. Apress Media, LLC is a California LLC and the sole member (owner) is Springer Science + Business Media Finance Inc (SSBM Finance Inc). SSBM Finance Inc is a **Delaware** corporation.

For information on translations, please e-mail booktranslations@springernature.com; for reprint, paperback, or audio rights, please e-mail bookpermissions@springernature.com.

Apress titles may be purchased in bulk for academic, corporate, or promotional use. eBook versions and licenses are also available for most titles. For more information, reference our Print and eBook Bulk Sales web page at http://www.apress.com/bulk-sales.

Any source code or other supplementary material referenced by the author in this book is available to readers on GitHub (https://github.com/Apress/Getting-Started-with-Containers-in-Azure). For more detailed information, please visit https://www.apress.com/gp/services/source-code.

Paper in this product is recyclable

Table of Contents

About the Author

Shimon Ifrah is a solution architect, writer, tech blogger, and author with over 15 years of experience in the design, management, and deployment of information technology systems, applications, and networks. In the last decade, Shimon has specialized in cloud computing and containerized applications for Microsoft Azure, Microsoft 365, Azure DevOps, and .NET. Shimon also holds over 20 vendor certificates from Microsoft, Amazon Web Services, VMware, Oracle, and Cisco. During his career in the IT industry, he has worked for some of the world's largest managed services and technology companies, assisting them in designing and managing systems used by millions of people every day. He is based in Melbourne, Australia.

About the Technical Reviewer

 **Kasam Shaikh** is a prominent figure in India's artificial intelligence landscape, holding the distinction of being one of the country's first four Microsoft MVPs in AI. Currently serving as a senior architect at Capgemini, Kasam boasts an impressive track record as an author, having authored five best-selling books focused on Azure and AI technologies. Beyond his writing endeavors, Kasam is recognized as a Microsoft certified trainer and influential tech YouTuber (@mekasamshaikh). He also leads the largest online Azure AI community, known as DearAzure—Azure INDIA and is a globally renowned AI speaker. His commitment to knowledge sharing extends to his contributions to Microsoft Learn, where he plays a pivotal role.

Within the realm of AI, Kasam is a respected subject matter expert in Generative AI for the Cloud, complementing his role as a senior cloud architect. He actively promotes the adoption of no-code and Azure OpenAI solutions and possesses a strong foundation in hybrid and cross-cloud practices. Kasam's versatility and expertise make him an invaluable asset in the rapidly evolving landscape of technology, contributing significantly to the advancement of Azure and AI.

In summary, Kasam Shaikh is a multifaceted professional who excels in both his technical expertise and knowledge dissemination. His contributions span writing, training, community leadership, public speaking, and architecture, establishing him as a true luminary in the world of Azure and AI.

## CHAPTER 1

Getting Started with Azure and Terraform

Introduction

Welcome to the first chapter of *Deploy Containers on Azure Using Terraform*. Since the release of the first edition of this book, many things have changed, and so I decided to do a complete rewrite of the original book and introduce the Terraform software and explain how it can help you simplify your deployments on Azure and, more important, how it can deploy fast and always produce the same results.

The focus of this book will be on how to use Terraform to deploy container services, infrastructure services, and other services on Azure using infrastructure as code (IaC).

Terraform is an open-source IaC tool developed by HashiCorp in order to simplify deployments of cloud infrastructure using descriptive code language.

Once the code is deployed to Azure, it can also be version controlled and shared for development purposes.

This chapter will focus on how to get started setting up your development environment to use Terraform and connect to Azure and on deploying a sample resource.

Based on the assumption that you already have a working knowledge of Terraform and Azure, this book will focus on teaching the fundamentals of these technologies.

To deploy resources to Azure using Terraform, there are a few tools I would recommend using to make your deployment journey smoother and easier.

If you already have a preferred working setup and have the latest version of Terraform and Azure command-line interface (CLI) installed and up and running, you don't have to use the setup outlined in this book, or the book recommended here.

© Shimon Ifrah 2024
S. Ifrah, *Getting Started with Containers in Azure*, https://doi.org/10.1007/978-1-4842-9972-2_1

Goals of This Chapter

The objectives of this chapter are to:

- install all the required tools and services of Terraform

- understand at a high level what configuring Terraform does

- authenticate to Azure using Azure CLI

- deploy an Azure resource group using Terraform

Tools and Services for the Setup

In the following sections, we will go over the tools and services needed to deploy infrastructure to Azure using Terraform. These resources can be run on Windows, macOS, and Linux operating systems.

The following tools and services are recommended:

- Visual Studio Code

- Visual Studio Code extensions

- Windows Subsystem for Linux (recommended but not essential)

- Azure command-line interface

- PowerShell 7

- Azure PowerShell Module

- Terraform

Visual Studio Code

Visual Studio Code (VS Code) is a lightweight source code editor developed by Microsoft that is free to download. It supports a wide range of programming languages and frameworks, including .NET, Python, Java, Node, PHP, HTML, and many more.

VS Code is currently one of the most popular source code editors because of the wide range of extensions it of offers to allow developers to write extensions that extend the functionality of the editor. In this book, we will use the Terraform extension.

Installing VS Code

VS Code is available for the Windows, macOS, and Linux operating systems. You can download all of these versions from the following URL: `https://code.visualstudio.com/download`.

Once you download the correct version for your system, go ahead and install it.

VS Code Extensions

VS Code extensions are core components that allow software and infrastructure developers to work smarter by complementing their capabilities with new features, functionality, and integrations.

Currently, the VS Code extensions library contains thousands of extensions that developers can use to produce cleaner and better code.

In this book, we will use a few extensions to produce code and infrastructure in Azure.

Installing VS Code Extensions

To install extensions in VS Code, take the following steps:

1. Open VS Code.

2. Click the "Extensions" icon, as shown in Figure 1-1.

Figure 1-1. *The VS Code "Extensions" icon*

To get the most out of this book and Terraform, what follows are a few VS Code extensions I would recommend installing that will help you become a great infrastructure developer.

- *Azure Terraform*: The official Microsoft VS Code extension for Terraform offers IntelliSense, linting, autocomplete, and ARM template support for Terraform configuration.

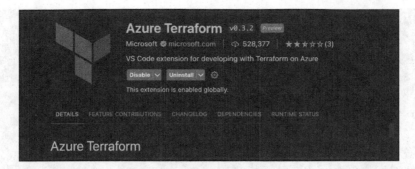

Figure 1-2. *The Azure Terraform VS Code extension*

- *HashiCorp Terraform*: HashiCorp, the company behind Terraform, has its own official VS Code extension that offers IntelliSense, syntax validation, syntax highlighting, code navigation, code formatting, code snippets, a Terraform module explorer, and Terraform commands.

Figure 1-3. *The HashiCorp Terraform VS Code extension*

- *Azure Account*: Another official Microsoft extension, Azure Account simplifies the connectivity process between VS Code and Azure. It allows developers to connect to multiple Azure subscriptions and manage Azure resources.

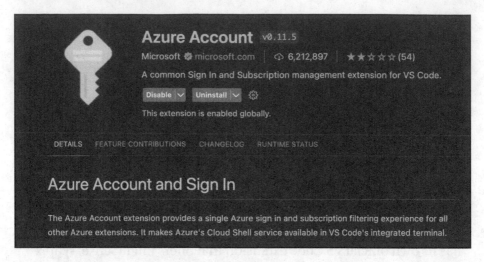

Figure 1-4. *The Azure Account VS Code extension*

- *PowerShell*: Microsoft's PowerShell VS Code extension offers support for PowerShell within VS Code and allows writing and debugging PowerShell scripts. The extension also offers the classic PowerShell Integrated Scripting Environment theme.

Figure 1-5. *The PowerShell VS Code extension*

- *Linter*: This extension offers linting capabilities that analyze and check the code written for errors and bugs. It also offers linting capabilities for YAML files used by Kubernetes code deployments.

To lint YAML Ain't Markup Language, or YAML, files, make sure you install the YAMLint package for macOS or Linux.

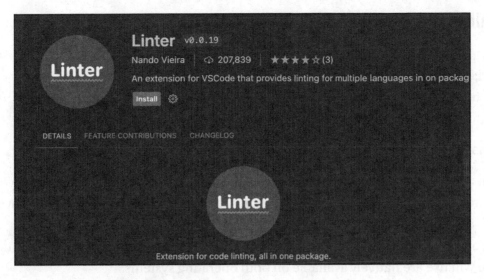

Figure 1-6. *The Linter VS Code extension*

The extensions just described will help you get started using Azure and Terraform very quickly. Make sure you have all of them installed.

Windows Subsystem for Linux

If you're planning on using a Windows operating system to deploy resources to Azure using Terraform, I recommend you go with Windows Subsystem for Linux (WSL) if you have enough Linux Shell skills.

WSL allows us to run Linux distributions natively on Windows 11 and Windows Server. It provides a convenient development environment for DevOps and Terraform specifically because of its:

- seamless integration with the Windows operating system, allowing us to use all the native Linux tools and scripts without using a different system

- native command-line experience, giving us access to Linux packages and utilities

- access to DevOps tools that are available on Linux only

By using WSL, developers and engineers can benefit from the strength of both operating systems and utilize all the tools and services they offer under a single system.

Installing WSL on Windows 11

Since the release of WSL back in 2016, the installation process has been simplified tenfold; now, installing WSL is just a matter of running a single command.

To install WSL on a Windows 11 computer, open PowerShell or a Windows Command terminal as an administrator and run the following command:

```
wsl-install
```

This command will install and enable all the features that make WSL work on your computer and install the Ubuntu distribution of Linux, which is the default, but you can change it.

If you're using macOS or Linux, there is no need to change anything, as all the tools that we will use are natively available on both operating systems.

Azure CLI

The next tool that we need to install is the Azure CLI command-line interface, which will allow us to manage Azure using commands. Azure CLI is a cross-platform tool that is available on all operating systems.

Installing Azure CLI on Windows with WinGet

To install Azure CLI on a computer running Windows 11, open PowerShell in administrator mode and run the following command:

```
winget install -e --id Microsoft.AzureCLI
```

This command uses WinGet, which is Windows's package manager that allows us to install tools and applications directly from the command line.

Installing Azure CLI on Linux

To install Azure CLI on a computer running Linux, visit the following page and select the Linux distribution you're running:

```
https://learn.microsoft.com/en-us/cli/azure/install-azure-cli
```

If you're using Ubuntu Linux, you can install Azure CLI using the following single command:

```
curl -sL https://aka.ms/InstallAzureCLIDeb | sudo bash
```

Installing Azure CLI on macOS

To install Azure CLI on a macOS using Homebrew, run the following command from the macOS terminal:

```
brew update && brew install azure-cli
```

PowerShell 7

Microsoft PowerShell is a cross-platform command-line utility that allows us to automate tasks using commands and scripts, and it is available on Windows, Linux, and macOS.

With PowerShell, we can install the Azure PowerShell module and manage Azure resources directly from the command line using cmdlets or scripts.

The main selling point of PowerShell 7 is its cross-platform support, which contributed to the program's success and widened its limited exposure, previously being available for Windows environments only.

PowerShell 7 can be installed on all platforms using different methods. For the sake of simplicity, I will just go over one method for each platform. For more information about the installation options, visit PowerShell's official website at https://github.com/PowerShell/PowerShell.

Installing PowerShell 7 on Windows

The recommended way to install PowerShell 7 on a Windows computer is to use the Windows Package Manager WinGet command-line tool. WinGet allows us to install, upgrade, and remove applications and tools like PowerShell directly from the command line and comes preinstalled on Windows 11 and recent versions of Windows 10.

To install PowerShell 7, open a Windows command terminal or PowerShell 5.1, which is also installed on Windows 10 and 11 by default, and run the following cmdlet:

```
winget install --id Microsoft.Powershell --source winget
```

To install the preview edition of PowerShell, run this command:

```
winget install --id Microsoft.Powershell.Preview --source winget
```

If you already have PowerShell 7 installed on your computer and would like to update it to the latest version, run the following command to check for updates:

```
winget update
```

To update all applications using WinGet, run the next command:

```
winget update -all
```

To update only PowerShell, you can run:

```
winget update Microsoft.PowerShell
```

Note that in some cases, you might need to uninstall PowerShell 7 before installing a new version with WinGet. To uninstall PowerShell 7, run the following cmdlet:

```
winget uninstall Microsoft.PowerShell
```

Once the previous version is uninstalled, install PowerShell 7 with the command that follows:

```
winget install Microsoft.PowerShell
```

Installing PowerShell 7 on macOS

The recommended way to install PowerShell 7 on macOS is by using Homebrew, which is a package manager for macOS. Like WinGet, Homebrew takes care of the installation process and allows us to install, update, and remove applications.

If you need to install Homebrew, open the Terminal application on your macOS and run the following command:

```
/bin/bash -c "$(curl -fsSL https://raw.githubusercontent.com/Homebrew/install/HEAD/install.sh)"
```

After the Homebrew installation is completed, close and reopen the Terminal and run the following command to install PowerShell 7:

```
brew install --cask powershell
```

Once PowerShell 7 is installed, you can start using it by typing "pwsh." The pwsh command starts PowerShell and allows you to run PowerShell cmdlets or scripts.

To update all applications, including PowerShell, on macOS, run the following command:

```
brew update
```

After the command is finished, run the following command to start the update process:

```
brew upgrade
```

When the Homebrew update is completed, it will display a summary report of the updated packages, including PowerShell 7.

Installing PowerShell 7 on Linux

PowerShell can be installed on almost all Linux distributions. Here, I will show how to install it on Ubuntu 22.04.

To install PowerShell, run the following commands from a bash terminal:

```
sudo apt-get update

sudo apt-get install -y wget apt-transport-https software-properties-common

wget -q
"https://packages.microsoft.com/config/ubuntu/$(lsb_release -rs)/packages-microsoft-prod.deb"

sudo dpkg -i packages-microsoft-prod.deb

rm packages-microsoft-prod.deb
packages.microsoft.com

sudo apt-get update

sudo apt-get install -y powershell
```

Once the installation is complete, you can start PowerShell by using the following command: pwsh. From this point forward, all PowerShell cmdlets will be the same on all operating systems.

Terraform

Now that we have all the tools we need to get started using Microsoft Azure and DevOps, it's time to install Terraform and begin the process.

Terraform is the most popular and widely used IaC software development tool available on the market and is considered an industry standard for infrastructure deployment.

It's also the oldest tool for infrastructure deployment and has been around for many years. Terraform supports most major cloud providers, like AWS, or Amazon Web Services, and GCP, or Google Cloud Platform.

Terraform uses the concept of domain-specific language, also known as HashiCorp Configuration Language. The idea behind the language is to use a declarative approach to infrastructure code.

In the declarative approach, we define the desired state of the infrastructure and let Terraform handle the deployment and configuration.

A High-Level Example of Terraform

The following is an example of code we can use to create an Azure Resource Group using Terraform:

```
# main.tf
provider "azurerm" {
  features {}
}
resource "azurerm_resource_group" "example" {
  name     = "Apress-ch01"
  location = "West Europe"
}
```

In this example, we have a Terraform configuration file called `main.tf`.

It is important to note that all Terraform configuration files need to use the `.TF` file extension in order to be deployed by Terraform.

In Terraform, a provider has all the domain-specific code to deploy resources to a cloud provider like Azure. Each cloud provider has its own Terraform provider. The Azure Terraform provider is called Azure Resource Manager (Azure RM).

The following code declares that we are using the Microsoft Azure Terraform provider.

```
provider "azurerm" {
  features {}
}
```

Next, we will tell Terraform to create a resource group in the Azure Web Europe data center. The name of the resource group will be Apress-ch01. Once we run the code, Terraform will go ahead and deploy the resource group.

We will go over the process for setting up and deploying a resource shortly. The previous code is just meant to serve as a high-level example of how Terraform deploys infrastructure

Now that we have learned a bit about Terraform, let's take a look at how to install it. Terraform is available for Linux, macOS, and Windows systems. My recommendation would be to use Terraform on Linux, macOS, or WSL. Because many DevOps tools are available natively on Linux and macOS, using Windows won't produce the best development results.

Installing Terraform on macOS

The method I would recommend to install Terraform on a macOS is to use a package manager; in our case, it is best to use Brew.

To install Terraform using Brew, you can use the next couple of commands on your macOS terminal.

First, install the HashiCorp repository using the tap command: `brew tap hashicorp/tap`. Then, to install Terraform, run this command:

```
brew install hashicorp/tap/terraform.
```

If you already have Terraform installed and want to update it to the latest version, you can take the following steps.

First, update Brew using the update command: `brew update`. Once Brew is updated, run this command: `brew upgrade hashicorp/tap/terraform`.

Now Terraform is ready to go. To check which version of Terraform is installed on your machine, run `terraform -version`.

Enabling Terraform Tab Completion on macOS

To enable tab completion for Terraform, first make sure you have the Bash profile configured by running the following command: `Touch ~/bashrc`. Then, run this command:

```
terraform -install-autocomplete.
```

Installing Terraform on Linux

In this section, I will install Terraform only on Ubuntu; if you're running a different Linux distribution, you can go to the following URL to get the version you need: `https://developer.hashicorp.com/terraform/tutorials/aws-get-started/install-cli`.

Terraform is available for the following Linux distributions:

- CentOS/RHEL
- Fedora
- Amazon Linux

Installing Terraform on Ubuntu

To install Terraform on Ubuntu, we first need to install the HashiCorp package repository, which we can do here:

```
wget -O- https://apt.releases.hashicorp.com/gpg | sudo gpg --dearmor -o
/usr/share/keyrings/hashicorp-archive-keyring.gpg
```

Then we need to install the GPG security signature using the following command:

```
echo "deb [signed-by=/usr/share/keyrings/hashicorp-archive-keyring.gpg]
https://apt.releases.hashicorp.com $(lsb_release -cs) main" | sudo tee
/etc/apt/sources.list.d/hashicorp.list
```

The last command will install Terraform:

```
sudo apt update && sudo apt install terraform
```

Enabling Terraform Tab Completion on Ubuntu

To enable tab completion for Terraform on Linux Ubuntu, first make sure you have the Bash profile configured by running the following command:

```
Touch ~/bashrc
```

Then, run this command:

```
terraform -install-autocomplete
```

Installing Terraform on Windows

The recommended method for installing Terraform on Windows is to use a package manager, and to do this we will again use WinGet.

To search for Terraform with WinGet, open a PowerShell terminal and run the following command:

```
winget search terraform
```

The output from the command is shown in the following. The version of Terraform we're looking for is 1.5.3.

```
Name                      Id                              Version Match Source
-----------------------------------------------------------------------------
Hashicorp Terraform       Hashicorp.Terraform     1.5.3    winget
```

Note   When the ID of the app shows "Vendor. AppName," it means that app is the official application.

To install Terraform, run this command:
```
Winget install Hashicorp.Terraform
```

Terraform Package Manager

Before we move on with, there is a tool I recommend you use to manage Terraform. This tool is optional but can help in managing Terraform across multiple deployments.

Note   Using tfenv is optional and not required to complete the labs in this book.

The tool I'm talking about is tfenv. It is a version manager for Terraform. Tfenv allows you to manage multiple versions of Terraform on your local computer (similar to the Python virtual environment).

The tfenv process of switching between Terraform environments is simple and allows us to maintain the compatibility of projects.

As I mentioned previously, this tool is only available on Linux and macOS; you will come across many tools like this.

Installing tfenv on macOS

To install tfenv on macOS, we'll use Homebrew with the brew command tool as shown in the following code:

```
brew install tfenv
```

In the next subsection, I will go over how to use tfenv.

Installing tfenv on Linux

To install tfenv on a Linux machine, use the following command, which uses Git to clone the source code of tfenv:

```
git clone --depth=1 https://github.com/tfutils/tfenv.git ~/.tfenv

echo 'export PATH=$PATH:$HOME/.tfenv/bin' >> ~/.bashrc
```

Note   Tfenv is not available in the Ubuntu package manager.

Tfenv is now installed on your computer.

How to Use tfenv

Now that we've tfenv installed on our computers, let's put it to the test and use it to manage different versions of Terraform.

To view all the available tfenv commands, run the following command:

```
Tfenv
```

The output will list all the available options, as shown in the following:

```
tfenv 3.0.0-18-g1ccfddb
Usage: tfenv <command> [<options>]

Commands:
    install     Install a specific version of Terraform
    use         Switch a version to use
    uninstall   Uninstall a specific version of Terraform
    list        List all installed versions
```

```
list-remote    List all installable versions
version-name   Print current version
init           Update environment to use tfenv correctly.
pin            Write the current active version to ./.terraform-version
```

As you can tell, using tfenv is simple, which makes it very handy for operating and managing the Terraform versions.

Let's start by downloading a version of Terraform by typing in the following command to view which versions are available:

```
Tfenv list-remote
```

What follows is the output of that command (note that I am only showing 14 of the versions included in the list):

```
1.6.0-alpha20230719
1.5.3
1.5.2
1.5.1
1.5.0
1.5.0-rc2
1.5.0-rc1
1.5.0-beta2
1.5.0-beta1
1.5.0-alpha20230504
1.5.0-alpha20230405
1.4.6
1.4.5
1.4.4
```

To install a specific version of Terraform, run the following command:

```
tfenv install 1.5.2
```

The command output follows. If you notice, it's being downloaded from Terraform directly.

```
Installing Terraform v1.5.2
Downloading release tarball from https://releases.hashicorp.com/
terraform/1.5.2/terraform_1.5.2_linux_amd64.zip
```

```
########################################################################
########################################################################
######################################### 100.0%
Downloading SHA hash file from https://releases.hashicorp.com/
terraform/1.5.2/terraform_1.5.2_SHA256SUMS
Downloading SHA hash signature file from https://releases.hashicorp.com/
terraform/1.5.2/terraform_1.5.2_SHA256SUMS.72D7468F.sig
```

To activate a version of Terraform, first list all the installed versions with a tfenv list, as follows:

```
* 1.5.3 (set by /home/shimon/.tfenv/version)
  1.5.2
  1.3.0
  1.1.8
```

To activate a different version of Terraform, run:

```
Tfenv use 1.5.2
```

If you check which version is active, it will show the following output:

```
  1.5.3
* 1.5.2 (set by /home/shimon/.tfenv/version)
  1.3.0
  1.1.8
```

As I mentioned at the beginning of this section, tfenv is an optional feature and it's not required to deploy infrastructure. You will find that there are many handy tools available to help us be more productive and efficient with our deployments; tfenv is just one of them.

Getting Started with Azure Infrastructure

At this stage, we have all the tools required to deploy infrastructure on Microsoft Azure. So let's get started and deploy something to Azure using Terraform.

Note   To deploy resources to Azure, you'll need an active Azure subscription.

Authenticating to Azure

The first step required to deploy resources to Azure is to authenticate, which we'll do using Azure CLI (PowerShell is not supported).

To authenticate to Azure, run the following command and click the resulting link to open the Azure portal login:

```
az login --use-device-code
```

If you have multiple Azure subscriptions, run the following command to find the ID of the subscription to which you're going to deploy resources and copy the subscription ID.

```
az account list --output table
```

Using the ID you copied, run the following command to set up the subscription:

```
az account set subscription "SUBSCRIPTIONNAME"
```

We are now authenticated and ready to deploy our first Azure resource.

In this example, we are going to deploy an Azure Resource Group using Terraform with the following code:

```
#1.Create_RG.tf
terraform {
  required_providers {
    azurerm = {
      source  = "hashicorp/azurerm"
    }
  }
}
provider "azurerm" {
  features {}
}
resource "azurerm_resource_group" "rg" {
  name     = "ApressAzureTerraform"
  location = "Australia Southeast"
}
```

The previous code starts with a declaration of the Azure Terraform provider. The Azure terraform provider is called azurerm.

19

We also have a provider features section where we can declare extra configuration items.

```
#1.Create_RG.tf
terraform {
  required_providers {
    azurerm = {
      source  = "hashicorp/azurerm"

    }
  }
}

provider "azurerm" {
  features {}
}
```

The second part of the code is the declaration of the resource group we're going to create and deploy to Azure.

We are deploying a resource group called ApressAzureTerraform in the Australia Southeast data center.

```
resource "azurerm_resource_group" "rg" {
  name     = "ApressAzureTerraform"
  location = "Australia Southeast"
}
```

Deploying Azure Infrastructure with Terraform

Now that we have a basic understanding of the code, let's deploy the resource group to Azure.

Terraform uses the following four commands to deploy, manage, and delete resources on any platform, not just Azure:

```
Terraform init
Terraform plan
Terraform apply
Terraform destroy
```

In the following deployment, we'll use all of these commands as we go through the cycle of creating and deleting resources from Azure.

The "Terraform Init" Command

We'll start by running the `terraform init` command, which will initiate and download the latest version of the Azure Terraform provider:

```
terraform init
```

Note   We can specify a Terraform provider by using the version option in the required_provider section.

The output of the command is as follows:

```
Initializing the backend...

Initializing provider plugins...
- Finding latest version of hashicorp/azurerm...
- Installing hashicorp/azurerm v3.66.0...
- Installed hashicorp/azurerm v3.66.0 (signed by HashiCorp)
```

Terraform has created a lock file called `.terraform.lock.hcl` to record the provider selections it made. Include this file in your version control repository so that Terraform can guarantee it makes the same selections by default when you run `"terraform init"` in the future.

The "Terraform Plan" Command

Before we go ahead and deploy the code, let's first use the `Terraform plan` command, which will show us what Terraform will do without deploying the code or making any changes.

The output is shown in the following, and as you can see in the `Plan` line, we've added one resource.

```
Terraform used the selected providers to generate the following execution
plan. Resource actions are indicated with the following symbols:
  + create
```

```
Terraform will perform the following actions:

  # azurerm_resource_group.example will be created
  + resource "azurerm_resource_group" "example" {
      + id       = (known after apply)
      + location = "australiasoutheast"
      + name     = "ApressAzureTerraform"
    }

Plan: 1 to add, 0 to change, 0 to destroy.
```

Note   It is essential that you review the changes carefully, as changes made by Terraform are irreversible.

The "Terraform Apply" Command

To deploy the resources, we'll use the following Terraform apply command to create a resource group:

Terraform apply

Let's now review the planned changes one more time and type "yes" to confirm.

```
Terraform used the selected providers to generate the following execution
plan. Resource actions are indicated with the following symbols:
  + create

Terraform will perform the following actions:

  # azurerm_resource_group.rg will be created
  + resource "azurerm_resource_group" "rg" {
      + id       = (known after apply)
      + location = "australiasoutheast"
      + name     = "ApressAzureTerraform"
    }

Plan: 1 to add, 0 to change, 0 to destroy.
```

```
Do you want to perform these actions?
  Terraform will perform the actions described above.
  Only 'yes' will be accepted to approve.

  Enter a value:
```

After a little time, Terraform will display a message saying that the resources were deployed successfully. The output of the message follows:

```
Apply complete! Resources: 1 added, 0 changed, 0 destroyed.
```

The "Terraform Destroy" Command

The final step in the Terraform deployment cycle is to delete the infrastructure we just deployed, which we'll do with the following destroy command:

```
Terraform destroy
```

Terraform will then again display a detailed configuration message outlining the changes and their impact on the infrastructure. It is critical that you review these changes carefully, especially when managing live and production resources.

```
Terraform used the selected providers to generate the following execution
plan. Resource actions are indicated with the following symbols:
  - destroy

Terraform will perform the following actions:

  # azurerm_resource_group.rg will be destroyed
  - resource "azurerm_resource_group" "rg" {
      - id       = "/subscriptions/subidremoved /resourceGroups/
                    ApressAzureTerraform" -> null
      - location = "australiasoutheast" -> null
      - name     = "ApressAzureTerraform" -> null
      - tags     = {} -> null
    }

Plan: 0 to add, 0 to change, 1 to destroy.
```

```
Do you really want to destroy all resources?
  Terraform will destroy all your managed infrastructure, as shown above.
  There is no undo. Only 'yes' will be accepted to confirm.

  Enter a value:
```

If you are OK with the changes, type "yes" and Terraform will delete the resources outlined in the output of the destroy command.

Summary

This chapter covered the basics of getting started with Terraform and installing the tools required to use it. In the last section, we put all our learning into practice and deployed an Azure resource group using Terraform.

CHAPTER 2

Azure Web App for Containers

Introduction

We'll start this chapter by deploying services to Azure. The first service we're going to explore and deploy is Azure Web App for Containers. Using the knowledge we gained in Chapter 1, we will use VS Code, Azure CLI, and Terraform.

Azure Web App for Containers is a service that is part of Azure Web Apps that allows us to deploy web or mobile applications to Azure without the need to deploy the underlying infrastructure, like servers and storage, allowing us to focus only on deploying our applications and let Azure manage the rest.

The platform takes Azure Web Apps to the next level by allowing us to configure applications in Docker and ship them to Azure Web Apps but control all the runtime configuration within the application.

The service also supports Docker and other container technologies that allow us to package our applications and dependencies into a container image.

We have the choice to use multiple programming languages with the platform like:

- .NET

- Java

- Python

- Node

The deployment process also allows us to pull our images from container registries like Azure Container Registry (ACR) and Docker Hub or use source-code repositories like Azure Repos or GitHub.

25

© Shimon Ifrah 2024
S. Ifrah, *Getting Started with Containers in Azure*, https://doi.org/10.1007/978-1-4842-9972-2_2

Setting Up Web App for Containers

To get started deploying to Web App for Containers, review the Chapter 02 code in the repository for this book.

If you look at the code, you'll see that I have made some changes to how Terraform configuration should be used.

Provider Configuration

To simplify things and make the code more scalable and portable, I have created the following file: `provider.tf`.

The `provider` file contains all the details of the provider, and in our case, it's the Azure provider. By separating the provider configuration from the main configuration files, we centralize the provider configuration and reduce duplication.

The content of the `provider.tf` is:

```
terraform {
  required_providers {
    azurerm = {
      source  = "hashicorp/azurerm"
    }
  }
}
provider "azurerm" {
  features {}
}
```

Web App for Containers Configuration

Before we deploy an app to Web App for Containers, let's review the code and understand how it works.

Note   Terraform code is called configuration.

The first block in the configuration creates a resource group. The name of the block is "rg." Terraform doesn't care what you name it, but the naming does need to be consistent, and we will refer to it in the configuration.

```
resource "azurerm_resource_group" "rg" {
  name     = "ApressAzureTerraformCH02"
  location = "Australia Southeast"
}
```

The second piece of code, detailed in the following, creates a Linux Service plan called "Linux with P1v2 plan."

```
resource "azurerm_service_plan" "appservice" {
  name                = "Linux"
  resource_group_name = azurerm_resource_group.rg.name
  location            = azurerm_resource_group.rg.location
  os_type             = "Linux"
  sku_name            = "P1v2"
}
```

These two blocks of code define the Docker image that will be used in the Web App for Containers and the settings that are needed for it to run.

Note   Later on in the book, we will create a private container register in Azure and use it for deployments.

The last block of code, outlined in the following, creates the actual app that will be deployed to Web App for Containers. The important parts in the configuration are in the applications_stack and the app_settings blocks.

```
resource "azurerm_linux_web_app" "webapp" {
  name                = "ApressTFWebApp"
  resource_group_name = azurerm_resource_group.rg.name
  location            = azurerm_resource_group.rg.location
  service_plan_id     = azurerm_service_plan.appservice.id
```

```
site_config {
    always_on       = "true"
    application_stack {
        docker_image_name     = "httpd:latest"
        docker_registry_url = "https://index.docker.io/"

    }
}
    app_settings = {
        "DOCKER_ENABLE_CI" = "true"
}
}
```

The deployment that we're using is not overly complicated but does have all the moving parts needed to run an application on Web App for Containers.

The "Terraform Plan" Command

Before deploying the code, it is a good idea to explore the Terraform plan command. The job of this command is to do the following tasks:

- *Dependency analysis*: This analyzes the Terraform configuration files and code maps all resources, data sources, and modules that are needed for the deployment.

- *State analysis*: The state analysis checks if an existing state file exists (terraform.tfstate) and determine the current state of the infrastructure.

- *Resource Comparison*: This compare the desired state defined in the configuration files with the current state recorded in the state file (terraform.tfstate).

- *Execution Plan*: Once the dependency, state, and resource analyses are done, Terraform will generate this plan that outlines how the infrastructure will look and which actions need to be achieved (add, modify, or delete).

- *Output*: The final stage of this command is to display the execution plan and show which action will be taken against which resources.

The purpose of the `Terraform plan` command is to preview the planned changes before applying them and review their potential impact on the infrastructure.

When running a plan command, we need to navigate to the directory containing the Terraform configuration files and issue the following command:

```
terraform plan
```

The plan command will run the previous steps against every configuration file that ends with the .tf extension.

The Terraform State File

The Terraform state file acts as a recordkeeping mechanism for tracking the resources Terraform manages and their current state.

The key functions of this file you need to know about are:

- *Mapping the file's resources*: Mapping the resources listed in the file (`terraform.tfstate`) and the resources in Azure is the purpose of this file. If the configuration of Azure resources is different, Terraform will try to "fix" it and give it the same configuration as those in the state files by deleting or removing those resources that can be risky.

- *Mapping*: The state file holds information about the resource type; name; provider; and attributes like DNS, IP Address, and so on.

- *Locking*: In a production environment, the state files should be hosted in centralized storage so that multiple members can access them and make changes to their infrastructure without overwriting their configuration. To prevent overwriting, Terraform can lock the state files when changes are made by a single user. We'll learn how to use a remote state file later on.

- *Remote state*: By default, the state file is stored locally; however, in a production environment the best practice is to store it in remote storage and allow collaboration.

- *Sensitive data*: The state file should be excluded from source control storage because it contains sensitive data like passwords, API (application programming interface) keys, and more. When using a remote state file, the storage should be encrypted.

Deploying Web App for Containers

Now that we understand a bit more about the Terraform plan process and how the Terraform state file works, it's time to deploy our Web App for Containers application.

We deploy resources to Azure using the `Terraform apply` command. This command uses the Terraform configuration file and creates or modifies resources in Azure. The command does exactly when the it says it will do.

Before making any changes, Terraform will display the execution plan with the proposed changes and will always ask for confirmation before proceeding with the changes.

Note   To skip the confirmation approval step, we can use auto-approve, which will work with the "plan," "apply," and "destroy" commands.

When using the Terraform `apply` command in a production environment, always review the execution plan and ensure that you understand the changes Terraform will make before confirming.

Deploying the Code

To deploy our Web App for Containers app, we'll take the following steps:

1. Open the VS Code terminal and browse the for the folder where the Terraform configuration exists.

2. Log into Microsoft Azure using the following code:

   `az login --use-device-code`

3. If you have more than one Azure subscription, use the following command to set your subscription:

   `az account set --subscription "SUBSCRIPTIONID"`

Note   To list all your Azure subscription IDs using PowerShell, use the following command: "get-azSubscription | Select-Object Name, subscriptionid."

---

4. Run the Terraform init command to download the Azure
   provider.

The init command output should look like this:

```
Initializing the backend...

Initializing provider plugins...
- Reusing previous version of hashicorp/azurerm from the dependency lock file
- Using previously-installed hashicorp/azurerm v3.66.0

Terraform has been successfully initialized!

You may now begin working with Terraform. Try running "terraform plan" to see
any changes that are required for your infrastructure. All Terraform commands
should now work.

If you ever set or change modules or backend configuration for Terraform,
rerun this command to reinitialize your working directory. If you forget, other
commands will detect it and remind you to do so if necessary.
```

5. The next step is to run the following plan command and review
   the proposed infrastructure:

   ```
   Terraform plan
   ```

The output should look like this:

```
Terraform used the selected providers to generate the following execution
plan. Resource actions are indicated with the following symbols:
  + create

Terraform will perform the following actions:

  # azurerm_linux_web_app.webapp will be created
  + resource "azurerm_linux_web_app" "webapp" {
      + app_settings                       = {
          + "DOCKER_ENABLE_CI" = "true"
        }
      + client_affinity_enabled            = false
      + client_certificate_enabled         = false
      + client_certificate_mode            = "Required"
      + custom_domain_verification_id      = (sensitive value)
```

```
+ default_hostname                              = (known after apply)
+ enabled                                       = true
+ hosting_environment_id                        = (known after apply)
+ https_only                                    = false
+ id                                            = (known after apply)
+ key_vault_reference_identity_id               = (known after apply)
+ kind                                          = (known after apply)
+ location                                      = "australiasoutheast"
+ name                                          = "ApressTFWebApp"
+ outbound_ip_address_list                      = (known after apply)
+ outbound_ip_addresses                         = (known after apply)
+ possible_outbound_ip_address_list             = (known after apply)
+ possible_outbound_ip_addresses                = (known after apply)
+ public_network_access_enabled                 = true
+ resource_group_name                           = "ApressAzureTerraformCH02"
+ service_plan_id                               = (known after apply)
+ site_credential                               = (sensitive value)
+ zip_deploy_file                               = (known after apply)

+ site_config {
    + always_on                                 = true
    + container_registry_use_managed_identity   = false
    + default_documents                         = (known after apply)
    + detailed_error_logging_enabled            = (known after apply)
    + ftps_state                                = "Disabled"
    + health_check_eviction_time_in_min         = (known after apply)
    + http2_enabled                             = false
    + linux_fx_version                          = (known after apply)
    + load_balancing_mode                       = "LeastRequests"
    + local_mysql_enabled                       = false
    + managed_pipeline_mode                     = "Integrated"
    + minimum_tls_version                       = "1.2"
    + remote_debugging_enabled                  = false
    + remote_debugging_version                  = (known after apply)
    + scm_minimum_tls_version                   = "1.2"
    + scm_type                                  = (known after apply)
```

```
        + scm_use_main_ip_restriction              = false
        + use_32_bit_worker                        = true
        + vnet_route_all_enabled                   = false
        + websockets_enabled                       = false
        + worker_count                             = (known after apply)

        + application_stack {
            + docker_image_name        = "httpd:latest"
            + docker_registry_password = (sensitive value)
            + docker_registry_url      = "https://index.docker.io/"
            + docker_registry_username = (known after apply)
          }
      }
  }

# azurerm_resource_group.rg will be created
+ resource "azurerm_resource_group" "rg" {
    + id       = (known after apply)
    + location = "australiasoutheast"
    + name     = "ApressAzureTerraformCH02"
  }

# azurerm_service_plan.appservice will be created
+ resource "azurerm_service_plan" "appservice" {
    + id                          = (known after apply)
    + kind                        = (known after apply)
    + location                    = "australiasoutheast"
    + maximum_elastic_worker_count = (known after apply)
    + name                        = "Linux"
    + os_type                     = "Linux"
    + per_site_scaling_enabled    = false
    + reserved                    = (known after apply)
    + resource_group_name         = "ApressAzureTerraformCH02"
    + sku_name                    = "P1v2"
    + worker_count                = (known after apply)
  }

Plan: 3 to add, 0 to change, 0 to destroy.
```

The `plan` command is important and you should always take a few minutes to review the code. More specifically, always review the last line of the output that shows the planned changes for the action.

In our case, the plan command will add the following three simple instructions: `Plan: 3 to add, 0 to change, 0 to destroy`. However, in existing environments, the output might show only the change and destroy instructions; make sure you go through the list of changes and understand them before proceeding to the `apply` command.

6. Next, we'll run the following command:

```
terraform apply
```

The output of this command will be similar to that of the `plan` command. However, it will also include the following output plus confirmation:

```
Plan: 3 to add, 0 to change, 0 to destroy.

Do you want to perform these actions?
  Terraform will perform the actions described above.
  Only 'yes' will be accepted to approve.

  Enter a value:
```

I will go ahead and type "yes" here and let Terraform create the web application as per the configuration.

The Terraform application output is shown in the following code. The time it takes to create the infrastructure depends on the number of resources in the configuration. In our case, it should take less than a minute to complete the deployment.

```
azurerm_resource_group.rg: Creating...
azurerm_resource_group.rg: Creation complete after 1s [id=/subscriptions/
subid/resourceGroups/ApressAzureTerraformCH02]
azurerm_service_plan.appservice: Creating...
azurerm_service_plan.appservice: Creation complete after 7s [id=/
subscriptions/subid/resourceGroups/ApressAzureTerraformCH02/providers/
Microsoft.Web/serverfarms/Linux]
azurerm_linux_web_app.webapp: Creating...
azurerm_linux_web_app.webapp: Still creating... [10s elapsed]
azurerm_linux_web_app.webapp: Still creating... [20s elapsed]
```

```
azurerm_linux_web_app.webapp: Still creating... [30s elapsed]
azurerm_linux_web_app.webapp: Creation complete after 33s [id=/
subscriptions/subid/resourceGroups/ApressAzureTerraformCH02/providers/
Microsoft.Web/sites/ApressTFWebApp]

Apply complete! Resources: 3 added, 0 changed, 0 destroyed.
```

Now, the web app has been deployed and we can open the properties of the web app in the Azure portal and click the URL to see it in action.

The output of the web app is shown in Figure 2-1.

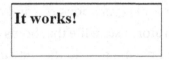

Figure 2-1. *Httpd default home page*

In our deployment, we're using the httpd Docker image, which runs the Apache Web Server, and it displays the default home page.

You can find the web app URL in the Azure portal by taking the following steps:

1. Open the Azure portal using the following URL: https://portal.
    azure.com.

2. Open the ApressTFWebApp web app.

3. Click the "Default domain," as shown in Figure 2-2.

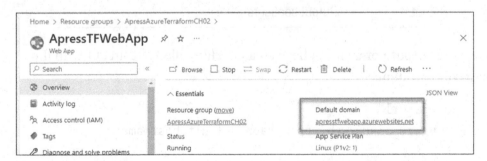

Figure 2-2. *Web app URL*

Terraform Output

I have to say that retrieving the web app URL required a few clicks, opening a web browser, and logging into the portal. To make our lives a bit easier, Terraform can also output the same information we retrieved from the browser on the output screen after deploying the application.

The purpose of the output command is to display information about the deployment on our screen without requiring us to open the portal to look for it. After all, Terraform already has all the information about our deployment, so outputting it to the screen is simple.

The Terraform output command is very powerful and allows us to retrieve deployment values from the Terraform state file that holds all the attributes. It also provides access to values without having to read the state file directly.

Creating an Output File

To use the output command, I recommend that you centralize all the output commands in one file called output.tf.

As a reminder, so far in our Web App for Containers we have the following files:

File Name	Details
webapp.tf	Main Web Apps for Containers configuration file
Provider.tf	Azure provider configuration file
Output.tf	Output configuration file

To use the output command, I have created a file called output.tf with the following configuration:

```
output "web_app_url" {
  value = azurerm_linux_web_app.webapp.default_hostname
}
```

In the configuration, I declared one output value would be called web_app_url with the Azure Web App default hostname value.

To view the hostname of the deployed web app, we can run the `terraform apply` command as normal or output the value postdeployment using:

```
terraform output
```

The following output shows the web app URL we get when we run the `Terraform apply` command:

```
azurerm_resource_group.rg: Refreshing state... [id=/subscriptions/subid /
resourceGroups/ApressAzureTerraformCH02]
azurerm_service_plan.appservice: Refreshing state... [id=/subscriptions/
subid/resourceGroups/ApressAzureTerraformCH02/providers/Microsoft.Web/
serverfarms/Linux]
azurerm_linux_web_app.webapp: Refreshing state... [id=/subscriptions/subid/
resourceGroups/ApressAzureTerraformCH02/providers/Microsoft.Web/sites/
ApressTFWebApp]

Changes to Outputs:
  + web_app_url = "apresstfwebapp.azurewebsites.net"

You can apply this plan to save these new output values to the Terraform
state, without changing any real infrastructure.

Do you want to perform these actions?
  Terraform will perform the actions described above.
  Only 'yes' will be accepted to approve.

  Enter a value: yes

Apply complete! Resources: 0 added, 0 changed, 0 destroyed.

Outputs:

web_app_url = "apresstfwebapp.azurewebsites.net"
```

The previous example shows one output; however, in more complex deployments, we could output almost any attribute in the deployment.

Using a Git Ignore File with Terraform

Before we start adding more code and configuration, I'd like to take a moment to discuss the importance of using a `.gitignore` file with Terraform, in case you're planning to use source control systems like GitHub or Azure Repos to store your code.

Storing state files in the `.terraform` directory isn't recommended, as these files should be protected and encrypted.

To protect your source code, I recommended using a `.gitignore` file in your repository and exclude a number of files. With a `.gitignore` file, we tell Git which files should be ignored and not tracked by Git.

To create a `.gitignore` file in our repository, we can create one by using the following command. The command should be executed in the same directory as your repository.

```
touch .gitignore
```

To exclude Terraform configuration files, I use the following configuration:

```
# Ignore Terraform state files
*.tfstate
*.tfstate.*

# Ignore .terraform directory, used to store plugins and state snapshots
.terraform/

# Ignore any local backup files
*~

# Ignore logs
*.log

# Ignore Mac-specific files
.DS_Store

# Ignore Visual Studio Code settings
.vscode/

# Ignore Terraform plan output files
*.tfplan
```

```
# Ignore sensitive files with secrets or API keys
secrets.tfvars
*.pem

# Ignore any generated files or directories
/bin/
/out/
```

If the .gitignore file is working, you'll see the ignored files marked in white rather than green, as shown in Figure 2-3, indicating that they are not being tracked.

Adding files to the .gitignore file after they've been tracked won't remove them from the repository; it will only prevent future changes from being staged.

To stop tracking files that Git already tracks, use the following Git command:

```
Git rm --cached
```

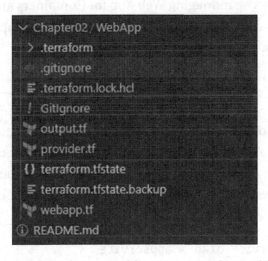

Figure 2-3. *Terraform file being ignored by Git, as indicated by being marked in white*

Using the Global Git Ignore File

We can also make a global .gitignore file that will apply to multiple repositories by taking the following steps:

1. Create a .gitignore file outside your repository indicating all the files you'd like Git to ignore and not track.

2. After adding the file, open a terminal window and find the repository with which you'd like to use the global file, then run the following command:

```
git config --global core.excludesfile ~/.gitignore_global
```

Cleaning Up Our Deployment

Before moving onto the next section, let's delete the Web App for Containers we just deployed using the following command:

```
Terraform destroy
```

Managing Web App for Containers

In this section, we'll focus on managing Web App for Containers and look into Azure features that can improve the deployment and management of apps running on Azure Web App for Containers.

Scaling

The first feature I want to touch on is the management of resources a Web App uses in terms of RAM and CPU. As I mentioned earlier, Terraform has the capability of managing almost any aspect of our deployment and scaling apps is one of them.

Regarding scaling, Azure Web Apps resources are managed at the app service plan resource we have in our configuration. The code is as follows:

```
resource "azurerm_service_plan" "appservice" {
  name                = "Linux"
  resource_group_name = azurerm_resource_group.rg.name
  location            = azurerm_resource_group.rg.location
  os_type             = "Linux"
  sku_name            = "P1v2"
}
```

If you look closely at the code, we manage the resources by assigning a Stock Keeping Unit (SKU) using the sku_name option. Currently, Azure offers ten app service plan options for Linux, as listed in Figure 2-4.

Name	Custom domain	Auto Scale	Daily backups	Staging slots	Zone Redundant	vNet integration	Single tenant system	Cost per hour	Cost per month
Dev/Test (For less demanding workloads)									
Free F1	-	N/A	N/A	N/A	·	·	·	Free	Free
Basic B1	✓	Manual	N/A	N/A	·	✓	·	0.026 AUD	19.044 AUD
Basic B2	✓	Manual	N/A	N/A	·	✓	·	0.051 AUD	37.085 AUD
Basic B3	✓	Manual	N/A	N/A	·	✓	·	0.10 AUD	73.167 AUD
Production (For most production workloads)									
Standard S1	✓	Rules	10	5	·	✓	·	0.165 AUD	120.275 AUD
Standard S2	✓	Rules	10	5	·	✓	·	0.33 AUD	240.55 AUD
Standard S3	✓	Rules	10	5	·	✓	·	0.659 AUD	481.099 AUD
Premium v2 P1V2	✓	Rules, Elastic	50	20	✓	✓	·	0.169 AUD	123.282 AUD
Premium v2 P2V2	✓	Rules, Elastic	50	20	✓	✓	·	0.336 AUD	245.561 AUD
Premium v2 P3V2	✓	Rules, Elastic	50	20	✓	✓	·	0.674 AUD	492.124 AUD

Figure 2-4. *App service plan options for Linux*

The process of adding more resources to an app service plan is called "scale up," and the opposite process is called "scale out."

To change an app service plan, we just need to change the sku_name value as follows, and then run Terraform apply.

```
resource "azurerm_service_plan" "appservice" {
  name                = "Linux"
  resource_group_name = azurerm_resource_group.rg.name
  location            = azurerm_resource_group.rg.location
  os_type             = "Linux"
  sku_name            = "S2"
}
```

Backing Up Web Apps

Microsoft Azure backs up all deployed web apps every hour by default. Azure offers two types of backups, automatic and custom.

Automatic backups are enabled by default at the following pricing tiers:

- basic

- standard

- premium

- isolated

41

With automatic backup, we are limited to 30 GB of backup, and backups run every hour without the option to run manual backups. Backups are retained for 30 days and cannot be downloaded to a local machine.

If you require a custom approach to your backups, you can use a custom backup by setting up a storage account to hold the backups. Once configured, the backup frequency and the retention period can be configured and changed.

Custom backups can be downloaded to an Azure storage blob.

Customizing Deployment

Before we move on to the next section, I'd like to show you how powerful Terraform is when it comes to customized deployments. In the following example, we're going to generate a random web app name for our application using Terraform.

To make our deployments easier and much more customized, Terraform has created a few providers that can help us generate random numbers, IDs, passwords, and more.

Going back to our Web App for Containers code, I'm now going to add a new code block that will generate a random number that I will use to make my web app name.

In the following code block, we'll use the random provider to generate a random number and use it to create the name of our web app. The provider details are available at https://registry.terraform.io/providers/hashicorp/random/latest/docs.

```
# Generate a random int
resource "random_integer" "random" {
  min = 1
  max = 20
}
```

In essence, this code will generate a random number between 1 and 20. I will use that number in the web app code block to form my web app name and URL.

```
resource "azurerm_linux_web_app" "webapp" {
  name                = "ApressTFWebApp${random_integer.random.result}"
  resource_group_name = azurerm_resource_group.rg.name
  location            = azurerm_resource_group.rg.location
  service_plan_id     = azurerm_service_plan.appservice.id
```

```
site_config {
    always_on        = "true"

    application_stack {
      docker_image_name       = "httpd:latest"
      docker_registry_url = "https://index.docker.io/"

    }
}
  app_settings = {
      "DOCKER_ENABLE_CI" = "true"
}

}
```

When I run the `Terraform apply` command, Terraform will generate a number and use it to form the web app URL, the result of which will be:

```
Apply complete! Resources: 4 added, 0 changed, 0 destroyed.

Outputs:

web_app_url = "apresstfwebapp18.azurewebsites.net"
```

The URL has now been formed and has the number 18 in it.

Variable Interpolation

You probably noticed that in the part of the previous code where we generated the number and formed the web app URL we used the following code to form the name:

```
"ApressTFWebApp${random_integer.random.result}"
```

This example is perfect for taking the opportunity to introduce the concept of variable interpolation.

In Terraform, variable interpolation is the process of using the values of variables within your Terraform configuration. Interpolation uses the following syntax:

```
${}
```

There are two types of variable interpolation:

- *Variable*: Used to reference the value of a variable.

- *Resource*: Used to reference the value of a resource (used in our web app configuration).

Securing Web App for Containers

In the final section of this chapter, we are going to focus on a few security features that are available to us and can be configured with Terraform, and I will provide examples of how to use them.

HTTPS

Azure Web Apps allows us to secure our applications using the HTTPS protocol, and by default, every deployment comes with an HTTPS URL enabled. To take this configuration a step further, we can also disable the use of HTTP using Terraform.

We can add the following line to the web app block if we want to make our web app support HTTPS only:

```
https_only = "true"
```

We can also enforce our web application to communicate using only the transport layer security (TLS) 1.2 HTTPS protocol and disable the use of unsecured TLS protocols like TLS 1.0.

The following line of code will set the minimum TLS protocol to 1.2:

```
minimum_tls_version = "1.2"
```

Another security feature that we can use is static IP restriction. By default, access to our web service is available to all IP (Internet protocol) addresses; however, we can limit which IP addresses have access to our application using IP restrictions.

The following code block adds restrictions to our web app from a static IP block:

```
ip_restriction {
    ip_address = "10.0.0.0/24"
    action     = "Allow"
# }
```

In the following code we will add the following security settings:

- HTTPS only

- Minimum TLS version

- IP restrictions

```
resource "azurerm_linux_web_app" "webapp" {
  name                = "ApressTFWebApp${random_integer.random.result}"
  resource_group_name = azurerm_resource_group.rg.name
  location            = azurerm_resource_group.rg.location
  service_plan_id     = azurerm_service_plan.appservice.id

  https_only = "true"

site_config {
    always_on           = "true"
    minimum_tls_version = "1.2"
    application_stack {
      docker_image_name    = "httpd:latest"
      docker_registry_url = "https://index.docker.io/"
    }

    ip_restriction {  # Use only if needed
    ip_address = "10.0.0.0/24"
      action    = "Allow"
    }

}

  app_settings = {
      "DOCKER_ENABLE_CI" = "true"
}

}
```

Private Endpoints

Private endpoints for web apps provide the ultimate security feature for securing web apps in Azure. These endpoints only allow access to web apps from private networks and block access to them by general users on the Internet.

A private network can be either an Azure Virtual Network (Vnet) or an on-premises network.

Private endpoints allow access to web apps from on-premises networks only or from Azure private networks.

To configure a private endpoint, we must create a Vnet and place the web app inside the network within the internal network interface controller (NIC).

In brief, Azure private endpoints use a private network interface that is available on a virtual network. When a private endpoint is being created, a private IP address is assigned to the web app instead of a public IP address.

We can also use access restrictions to white list or blacklist specific IP ranges or IP addresses.

To access a private endpoint from a Vnet, Azure uses a private domain name system (DNS) zone to resolve the private IP address.

Configuring Terraform for a Private Endpoint

The following Terraform configuration will create Web App for Containers using the same web app configuration we used earlier in this chapter, but here we'll instead configure the web app to use a private endpoint.

To do this configuration, we'll need the following resources:

- Azure Virtual Network

- Azure Subnet

- Virtual network connectivity

- A Private DNS zone

- a Private Endpoint

The configuration follows:

```
resource "azurerm_resource_group" "rg" {
  name     = "ApressAzureTerraformCH02.2"
  location = "Australia Southeast"
}

resource "random_integer" "random" {
  min = 1
  max = 20
}

resource "azurerm_virtual_network" "azvnet" {
  name                = "Vnet-WebAPP"
  location            = azurerm_resource_group.rg.location
  resource_group_name = azurerm_resource_group.rg.name
  address_space       = ["10.0.0.0/16"]
}

resource "azurerm_subnet" "webappssubnet" {
  name                 = "webappssubnet"
  resource_group_name  = azurerm_resource_group.rg.name
  virtual_network_name = azurerm_virtual_network.azvnet.name
  address_prefixes     = ["10.0.1.0/24"]
  delegation {
    name = "delegation"
    service_delegation {
      name = "Microsoft.Web/serverFarms"
    }
  }
}

resource "azurerm_subnet" "privatesubnet" {
  name                 = "privatesubnet"
  resource_group_name  = azurerm_resource_group.rg.name
  virtual_network_name = azurerm_virtual_network.azvnet.name
```

```
  address_prefixes      = ["10.0.2.0/24"]
  private_endpoint_network_policies_enabled = true
}

resource "azurerm_service_plan" "appservice" {
  name                = "Linux"
  resource_group_name = azurerm_resource_group.rg.name
  location            = azurerm_resource_group.rg.location
  os_type             = "Linux"
  sku_name            = "P1v2"
}

resource "azurerm_linux_web_app" "webapp" {
  name                = "ApressTFFront${random_integer.random.result}"
  resource_group_name = azurerm_resource_group.rg.name
  location            = azurerm_resource_group.rg.location
  service_plan_id     = azurerm_service_plan.appservice.id

  https_only = "true"

site_config {
    always_on         = "true"
    minimum_tls_version = "1.2"
    application_stack {
      docker_image_name    = "nginx:latest"
      docker_registry_url = "https://index.docker.io/"
    }
}

  app_settings = {
    "DOCKER_ENABLE_CI" = "true"
    vnet_route_all_enabled = "true"

}

}

resource "azurerm_app_service_virtual_network_swift_connection"
"vnetintegrationconnection" {
  app_service_id  = azurerm_linux_web_app.webapp.id
```

```
  subnet_id         = azurerm_subnet.webappssubnet.id
}

resource "azurerm_private_dns_zone" "dnsprivatezone" {
  name                  = "privatelink.azurewebsites.net"
  resource_group_name = azurerm_resource_group.rg.name
}

resource "azurerm_private_dns_zone_virtual_network_link" "dnszonelink" {
  name = "dnszonelink"
  resource_group_name = azurerm_resource_group.rg.name
  private_dns_zone_name = azurerm_private_dns_zone.dnsprivatezone.name
  virtual_network_id = azurerm_virtual_network.azvnet.id
}

resource "azurerm_private_endpoint" "privateendpoint" {
  name                  = "backwebappprivateendpoint"
  location              = azurerm_resource_group.rg.location
  resource_group_name = azurerm_resource_group.rg.name
  subnet_id             = azurerm_subnet.privatesubnet.id

  private_dns_zone_group {
    name = "privatednszonegroup"
    private_dns_zone_ids = [azurerm_private_dns_zone.dnsprivatezone.id]
  }

  private_service_connection {
    name = "privateendpointconnection"
    private_connection_resource_id = azurerm_linux_web_app.webapp.id
    subresource_names = ["sites"]
    is_manual_connection = false
  }
}
```

Disabling Public Access to the Web App

By default, once the web app is configured, public access to it is enabled. To disable
public access, we need to use the Azure portal.

Note   Disabling Azure Web App public access is not possible with Terraform.

To disable public access, open your newly created web app and click "Networking," as shown in Figure 2-5. Then, click "**Access restriction**" and uncheck "Allow public access," as shown in Figure 2-6.

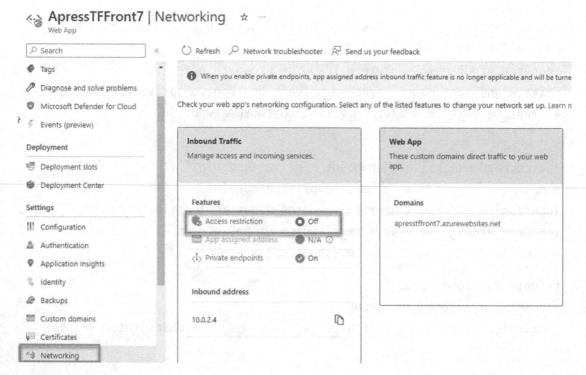

Figure 2-5. *Setting up access restriction*

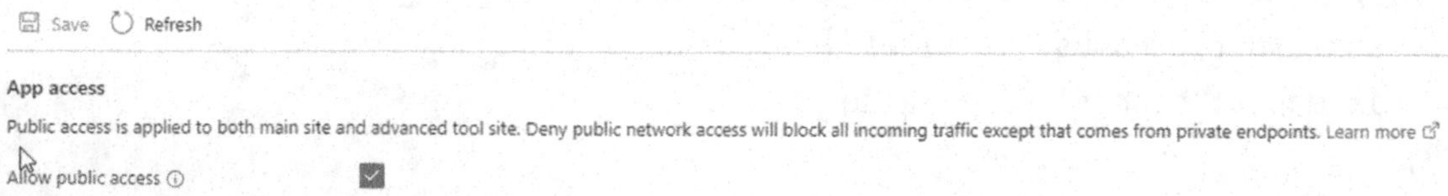

💾 Save ↻ Refresh

App access

Public access is applied to both main site and advanced tool site. Deny public network access will block all incoming traffic except that comes from private endpoints. Learn more ☐

Allow public access ⓘ   ☑

Figure 2-6. *Disabling public access*

We can also use the Azure CLI to disable public access with the following CLI command:

```
az resource update --resource-group ApressAzureTerraformCH02.2 --name
ApressTFFront7 --resource-type "Microsoft.Web/sites" --set properties.
publicNetworkAccess=Disabled
```

If someone on the Internet tries to open the web app after you've disabled public access, they'll receive the error message shown in Figure 2-7.

Figure 2-7. *Error message users will receive after public access has been disabled*

Summary

In this chapter, we covered the configuration and deployment of Azure Web App for Containers using Terraform. During the process, we learned about the following:

- the Terraform state file

- the global Git Ignore file

- backup web apps

- variable interpolation

- private endpoints

With these features, users should understand all the moving parts of a Terraform deployment.

As always, when deploying Terraform, it's important to take extra time to review the `terraform plan` command and ensure you understand the impact of the planned changes on the environment.

To control Azure resource costs, make sure you use the `terraform destroy` to delete the resources after you're done with the trial setup.

## CHAPTER 3

Azure Container Registry

Introduction

In this chapter, we're going to take a deep dive into Azure Container Registry (ACR) using Terraform. ACR is a private container registry service that enables us to store, manage, and secure container images in Azure.

The ACR service is an essential part of any modern application development life cycle and has advanced features that streamline and improve the development workflow.

ACR is also fully integrated with other Azure services like Azure Kubernetes Service (AKS), which we will also cover later in this book; Azure App Services; and Azure Function.

Key Features of Azure Container Images

Some of the most essential features of Azure Container Images are:

- *Security and privacy*: ACR offers secure infrastructure to store and manage container images with services like access control and role-based access control (RBAC).

- *Replication and optimization*: Besides security, ACR allows users to replicate container images across multiple Azure regions and data centers, which results in quicker deployment times and reduced costs of data transfer.

- *Seamless integration*: ACR seamlessly integrates with other Azure services like AKS and Azure Web Apps.

© Shimon Ifrah 2024
S. Ifrah, *Getting Started with Containers in Azure*, https://doi.org/10.1007/978-1-4842-9972-2_3

- *Role-based access control*: ACR uses the Azure Active Directory (AD) for RBAC and allows users to grant permissions easily to other users and groups in Azure without creating duplicate identities.

- *Automation*: ACR can be integrated with Azure DevOps pipelines and can automatically build and push images to ACR.

- *Private link*: ACR supports Azure Private Link, which allows users to make the registry available from internal networks connected to Azure and block any access to it from public networks.

- *Vulnerability scanning*: With ACR vulnerability scanning, users can scan images and detect security risks and vulnerabilities inside of the images.

Setting Up the Azure Container Registry

To get started with ACR, we'll dive straight in and do the following:

- Create an ACR using a Terraform configuration

- Pull a Docker image using the Azure CLI

- Build the image using Azure CLI

- Push the image to ACR

- Run the image directly from ACR

The main takeaway from the list of things we're going to do is that we're not going to use Docker to build and push our image using a Dockerfile. This is a capability of Azure CLI and can be done using ACR Tasks.

ACR Tasks is a suite of features in ACR that allows us to build container images for any platform. It also allows us to automate the build process using triggers like source code updates.

The advantage of ACR Tasks is that it eliminates the need for a local Docker engine installation and licensing for large businesses.

For example, the Docker `build` command in ACR Tasks is `az acr build`, which builds and pushes the image to an ACR repository.

Terraform Configuration

The following Terraform configuration can be used to create an ACR:

```
resource "azurerm_resource_group" "rg" {
  name     = "ApressAzureTerraformCH02"
  location = "australiasoutheast"
}

resource "azurerm_container_registry" "acr" {
  name                = "apresstfacr"
  resource_group_name = azurerm_resource_group.rg.name
  location            = azurerm_resource_group.rg.location
  sku                 = "Basic"
  admin_enabled       = true

  tags = {
    environment = "dev"
  }
}
```

In the repository under Chapter 3, you'll find the following files:

- `main.tf`: This file contains the configuration for ACR.

- `provider.tf`: This file features provider configuration details.

- `output.tf`: Output the ACR repository details.

Outputting Sensitive Information

Before we proceed, let's take a moment to learn about outputting sensitive information with Terraform. Since we're creating a private ACR that requires credentials to log in, we need to output the login details.

To do so, we'll use the following output file:

```
output "acr_url" {
  value = azurerm_container_registry.acr.login_server
}
```

```
output "admin_username" {
  value = azurerm_container_registry.acr.admin_username
  sensitive = true
}

output "admin_password" {
  value = azurerm_container_registry.acr.admin_password
  sensitive = true
}
```

The ACR details that we're outputting are:

- *ACR URL*: the public-facing URL that should be referenced when pushing an image to ACR.

- *Admin username*: the username that should be used to log in to ACR.

- *Admin password*: the password that will be used to log in in using the admin account.

Deploying the Azure Container Registry

Let's now deploy our ACR. To do so, we'll issue the following commands using our Terraform configuration file:

- `Terraform init`: initiates the configuration.

- `Terraform plan`: plans the deployment.

- `Terraform apply`: deploys the ACR registry.

The output of the `plan` command should look like this:

```
Terraform used the selected providers to generate the following execution
plan. Resource actions are indicated with the following symbols:
  + create

Terraform will perform the following actions:

  # azurerm_container_registry.acr will be created
  + resource "azurerm_container_registry" "acr" {
      + admin_enabled                    = true
```

```
      + admin_password               = (sensitive value)
      + admin_username               = (known after apply)
      + encryption                   = (known after apply)
      + export_policy_enabled        = true
      + id                           = (known after apply)
      + location                     = "australiasoutheast"
      + login_server                 = (known after apply)
      + name                         = "apresstfacr"
      + network_rule_bypass_option   = "AzureServices"
      + network_rule_set             = (known after apply)
      + public_network_access_enabled = true
      + resource_group_name          = "ApressAzureTerraformCH03"
      + retention_policy             = (known after apply)
      + sku                          = "Basic"
      + tags                         = {
          + "environment" = "dev"
        }
      + trust_policy                 = (known after apply)
      + zone_redundancy_enabled      = false
    }

  # azurerm_resource_group.rg will be created
  + resource "azurerm_resource_group" "rg" {
      + id       = (known after apply)
      + location = "australiasoutheast"
      + name     = "ApressAzureTerraformCH03"
    }

Plan: 2 to add, 0 to change, 0 to destroy.

Changes to Outputs:
  + acr_url        = (known after apply)
  + admin_password = (sensitive value)
  + admin_username = (sensitive value)
```

If you look at the output, you'll see that Terraform is going to create two resources, a resource group and an ACR.

Adding Tags

In case you didn't notice in the ACR code, I'm also tagging the ACR resource with a tag that uses the following code:

```
tags = {
    environment = "dev"
  }
```

Noticing the Output

Another important thing to notice in the deployment is the output. At the end of the deployment, you should see the following on the screen:

```
Apply complete! Resources: 2 added, 0 changed, 0 destroyed.
```

```
Outputs:
```

```
acr_url = "apresstfacr.azurecr.io"
admin_password = <sensitive>
admin_username = <sensitive>
```

Make note of the acr_url value, as we'll need it soon.

To view the username and output, run the following command:

```
terraform output -json
```

The output from the command should be:

```
{
  "acr_url": {
    "sensitive": false,
    "type": "string",
    "value": "apresstfacr.azurecr.io"
  },
  "admin_password": {
    "sensitive": true,
    "type": "string",
    "value": "PASSWORD SHOWS HERE"
  },
```

```
"admin_username": {
  "sensitive": true,
  "type": "string",
  "value": "apresstfacr"
}
```

The `terraform output -json` command outputs the sensitive information we marked in the configuration to the screen in JSON format.

Make sure to note the username and then proceed to the next section.

Building, Pushing, and Running Container Images with ASR Tasks

Now that we have a live ACR repository in Azure, it's time to test it, build a container image, and push it to it.

Using the details from the output, let's do the following:

1. *Create a Dockerfile*: We'll start by creating a local Dockerfile that will hold all the instructions of our image buildup.

   Creating the file is done in one step, and that's to pull the hello-world Docker image by using the following code:

   ```
   echo "FROM mcr.microsoft.com/hello-world" > Dockerfile
   ```

2. *Build a Docker image using the Azure ACR Tasks CLI:* Using the following Az CLI command, we're going to build our image using the Dockerfile we created. Make sure you change the registry address to your own ACR URL.

   ```
   az acr build --image ch03/image01:v1 --registry apresstfacr.
   azurecr.io --file Dockerfile .
   ```

   The following command output shows all the steps ACR Tasks takes in order to push the image to ACR:

   ```
   The login server endpoint suffix '.azurecr.io' is
   automatically omitted.
   ```

```
Packing source code into tar to upload...
Uploading archived source code from '/tmp/build_archive_
a50c78cc74ef40ebad7220c49518970e.tar.gz'...
Sending context (43.665 MiB) to registry: apresstfacr...
Queued a build with ID: cs1
Waiting for an agent...
Downloading source code...
Finished downloading source code
Using acb_vol_52a83d72-c559-4b69-86cd-7e11d920c69b as the
home volume
Setting up Docker configuration...
Successfully set up Docker configuration
Logging in to registry: apresstfacr.azurecr.io
Successfully logged into apresstfacr.azurecr.io
Executing step ID: build. Timeout(sec): 28800, Working
directory: '', Network: ''
Scanning for dependencies...
Successfully scanned dependencies
Launching container with name: build
Sending build context to Docker daemon  203.3MB
Step 1/1 : FROM mcr.microsoft.com/hello-world
latest: Pulling from hello-world
1b930d010525: Pulling fs layer
1b930d010525: Verifying Checksum
1b930d010525: Download complete
1b930d010525: Pull complete
Digest: sha256:92c7f9c92844bbbb5d0a101b22f7c2a7949e40f8ea90c
8b3bc396879d95e899a
Status: Downloaded newer image for mcr.microsoft.com/hello-
world:latest
 ---> fce289e99eb9
Successfully built fce289e99eb9
Successfully tagged apresstfacr.azurecr.io/ch03/image01:v1
Successfully executed container: build
Executing step ID: push. Timeout(sec): 3600, Working
directory: '', Network: ''
```

```
Pushing image: apresstfacr.azurecr.io/ch03/image01:v1,
attempt 1
The push refers to repository [apresstfacr.azurecr.io/ch03/
image01]
af0b15c8625b: Preparing
af0b15c8625b: Pushed
v1: digest: sha256:92c7f9c92844bbbb5d0a101b22f7c2a7949e40f8
ea90c8b3bc396879d95e899a size: 524
Successfully pushed image: apresstfacr.azurecr.io/ch03/
image01:v1
Step ID: build marked as successful (elapsed time in seconds:
2.956972)
Populating digests for step ID: build...
Successfully populated digests for step ID: build
Step ID: push marked as successful (elapsed time in seconds:
1.788662)
The following dependencies were found:
- image:
    registry: apresstfacr.azurecr.io
    repository: ch03/image01
    tag: v1
    digest: sha256:92c7f9c92844bbbb5d0a101b22f7c2a7949e40f8
    ea90c8b3bc396879d95e899a
  runtime-dependency:
    registry: mcr.microsoft.com
    repository: hello-world
    tag: latest
    digest: sha256:92c7f9c92844bbbb5d0a101b22f7c2a7949e40f8
    ea90c8b3bc396879d95e899a
  git: {}

Run ID: cs1 was successful after 10s
```

3. *Run the following command to check if the image was successfully pushed to the repository (optional):*

```
az acr repository list --name apresstfacr
```

In my case, the output shows the following single image; if multiple images are stored they will all be listed:

```
[
  "ch03/image01"
]
```

4. *Run the image*: The final step in this process is to check if the image can run once it has been uploaded to ACR. Once again, we're going to use ACR Tasks using the following command:

```
az acr run --registry apresstfacr.azurecr.io --cmd
'apresstfacr.azurecr.io/ch03/image01:v1' /dev/null
```

The output of the command follows:

```
Alias support enabled for version >= 1.1.0, please see
https://aka.ms/acr/tasks/task-aliases for more information.
Creating Docker network: acb_default_network, driver: 'bridge'
Successfully set up Docker network: acb_default_network
Setting up Docker configuration...
Successfully set up Docker configuration
Logging in to registry: apresstfacr.azurecr.io
Successfully logged into apresstfacr.azurecr.io
Executing step ID: acb_step_0. Timeout(sec): 600, Working
directory: '', Network: 'acb_default_network'
Launching container with name: acb_step_0
Unable to find image 'apresstfacr.azurecr.io/ch03/
image01:v1' locally
v1: Pulling from ch03/image01
1b930d010525: Pulling fs layer
1b930d010525: Verifying Checksum
1b930d010525: Download complete
1b930d010525: Pull complete
Digest: sha256:92c7f9c92844bbbb5d0a101b22f7c2a7949e40f8ea90c8b
3bc396879d95e899a
Status: Downloaded newer image for apresstfacr.azurecr.io/
ch03/image01:v1
```

```
Hello from Docker!
This message shows that your installation appears to be
working correctly.

To generate this message, Docker took the following steps:
 1. The Docker client contacted the Docker daemon.
 2. The Docker daemon pulled the "hello-world" image from the
    Docker Hub.
    (amd64)
 3. The Docker daemon created a new container from that image
    which runs the executable that produces the output you are
    currently reading.
 4. The Docker daemon streamed that output to the Docker
    client, which sent it to your terminal.

To try something more ambitious, you can run an Ubuntu
container with:
 $ docker run -it ubuntu bash

Share images, automate workflows, and more with a free
Docker ID:
 https://hub.docker.com/

For more examples and ideas, visit:
 https://docs.docker.com/get-started/

Successfully executed container: acb_step_0
Step ID: acb_step_0 marked as successful (elapsed time in
seconds: 11.035785)

Run ID: cs2 was successful after 14s
```

Pulling an Image from ACR

Now that we have a container image hosted in ACR, it's time to download it using the docker pull command. To pull an image from ACR, we will need to use the Docker CLI utility and the docker pull command.

As ACR tasks are only capable of building and pushing, we must use Docker CLI.

1. To get started, note your ACR URL, username, and passwords extracted from the output, and run the following command to log in to ACR:

```
docker login apresstfacr.azurecr.io
```

2. Provide the login details and continue.

3. After successfully authenticating to ACR, pull the image using the following command:

```
docker pull apresstfacr.azurecr.io/hello-world
```

ACR Pricing Tiers

When designing an ACR infrastructure, it's important that you understand the capabilities and pricing tiers that come with ACR.

As listed in the following table, ACR offers three pricing tiers. My recommendation is that you start with the basic tier and upgrade as needed.

	Basic	Standard	Premium
Daily cost	$0.167	$0.667	$1.667
Storage limit	10 GB	100 GB	500 GB
Web hooks	2	10	500
Replication	N/A	N/A	Available

In our ACR configuration, we set the pricing tier in the following SKU section:

```
name                 = "apresstfacr"
resource_group_name  = azurerm_resource_group.rg.name
location             = azurerm_resource_group.rg.location
sku                  = "Basic"
admin_enabled        = true
```

Managing the Azure Container Registry

In this section, we're going learn about ACR management and how we can use Azure CLI to manage an Azure container registry.

As we learned in the previous section, Azure CLI allows us to build and push images to an ACR registry, but instead of using the Azure portal we can also use the CLI for management purposes.

ACR Tasks

The following table lists several ACR tasks that are part of the Azure CLI command-line utility and describes what they do.

Command	Details
`az acr task logs --registry NAME -o table`	Displays ACR task logs.
`az acr task create`	Creates an ACR task.
`az acr task cancel-run`	Cancels specific ACR task runs.
`az acr task show`	Shows specific ACR task.
`az acr task run`	Manually starts an ACR task.
`az acr task update`	Updates an ACR task
`az acr task delete`	Deletes a task from ACR.

If, for example, we wanted to view all the ACR tasks that have finished running we could use the following command:

```
az acr task list-runs --registry apresstfacr.azurecr.io --resource-group
ApressAzureTerraformCH03  -o table

The login server endpoint suffix '.azurecr.io' is automatically omitted.
RUN ID    TASK    PLATFORM    STATUS      TRIGGER    STARTED              DURATION
-------   -----   ---------   --------    --------   ----------------     ----------
cs2               linux       Succeeded   Manual     08-09T04:30:56Z      00:00:14
cs1               linux       Succeeded   Manual     08-09T04:19:05Z      00:00:10
```

Running Azure CLI Commands with Terraform

In some scenarios, such as when Terraform can't manage the resources or is missing capabilities, you might need to run Azure CLI or Azure PowerShell commands after deployment in order to complete your configuration.

Terraform Null Resource

Because of the reasons just mentioned, Terraform has created the null resource that allows us to define actions like:

- running commands
- running scripts
- custom logic

The null_resource doesn't create any resource or infrastructure and act as a placeholder for us to use and complement deployment as a last resort.

A basic example of the null_resource is:

```
resource "null_resource" "example" {
  triggers = {
    timestamp = timestamp()
  }

  provisioner "local-exec" {
    command = "echo Resource created at ${timestamp()}"
  }
}
```

This code can be used with any Terraform configuration file to run scripts or commands.

To use the null_resource with our configuration, for example, we can add the following code and run the following Azure CLI Tasks command:

```
az acr task list-runs --registry apresstfacr.azurecr.io --resource-group
ApressAzureTerraformCH03  -o table
```

The Terraform configuration is:

```
resource "null_resource" "run-commands" {

  provisioner "local-exec" {
    command = <<EOT
      az acr task list-runs --registry ${azurerm_container_registry.acr.
      name}  --resource-group ${azurerm_resource_group.rg.name}  -o table
    EOT
  }
}
```

In the basic example, we're using the provisioners model with local-exec options that run the code on the system Terraform is operating; in our case, that's our local machine.

We can also use Terraform variables in the code without hard-coding the ACR registry name and the Azure resource group.

To use a variable, I'm choosing the ${} syntax and referencing the details needed by the Azure CLI command to run.

The output from the null_resource and the command is:

```
null_resource.run commands: Creating...
null_resource.run-commands: Provisioning with 'local-exec'...
null_resource.run-commands (local-exec): Executing: ["/bin/sh" "-c" "
az acr task list-runs --registry apresstfacr  --resource-group
ApressAzureTerraformCH03  -o table\n"]
null_resource.run-commands (local-exec):
RUN ID    TASK    PLATFORM    STATUS    TRIGGER    STARTED
  DURATION
null_resource.run-commands (local-exec):
--------  ------  ----------  ---------  ---------  --------------------
  ----------
null_resource.run-commands (local-exec):
cs2              linux      Succeeded  Manual     00:00:14
null_resource.run-commands (local-exec):
cs1              linux      Succeeded  Manual     00:00:10
null_resource.run-commands: Creation complete after 1s [id=3069836889725941298]
```

The full Terraform configuration is:

```
resource "azurerm_resource_group" "rg" {
  name     = "ApressAzureTerraformCH03"
  location = "australiasoutheast"

}

resource "azurerm_container_registry" "acr" {
  name                = "apresstfacr"
  resource_group_name = azurerm_resource_group.rg.name
  location            = azurerm_resource_group.rg.location
  sku                 = "Basic"
  admin_enabled       = true

  tags = {
    environment = "dev"
  }

}

resource "null_resource" "run-commands" {

  provisioner "local-exec" {
    command = <<EOT
      az acr task list-runs --registry ${azurerm_container_registry.acr.
      name}  --resource-group ${azurerm_resource_group.rg.name}  -o table
    EOT
  }
}
```

Securing ACR

In the last section of this chapter, we're going to focus on the security features of ACR, which we can implement using Terraform with the help of other Azure services.

In this section, we're going to deploy an ACR with the following features:

- Azure Key Vault with premium tier

- Key Vault access policy

- Azure AD service principal account

- Enabling of ACR encryption

- Enabling of soft delete with seven days' retention

- Purge protection

- Enabling of disk encryption

Terraform Data Sources

We're going to use Terraform data sources for the first time in order to read information from existing Azure data sources and resources.

We're also going to use the Terraform data sources to read and reference Azure data sources like TenantId, look up usernames, and more.

Data sources use a resource called data source, which we declare like this:

```
data "azuread_service_principal" "serviceprincipal" {
  display_name = "acr-admin"
}
```

In this example, we're looking up the service principal ID of an identity object called acr-admin.

In the configuration code in the next section, we're going to use data sources multiple times to reference ID and configuration items of resources in Azure and in the actual Azure configuration.

Securing Our ACR Configuration

To get us started understanding our ACR configuration, I will go over some of the configuration blocks that make up this deployment and explain them.

The following code block reads the Azure client information using a data source; the reason we call this data source is to grab the Azure tenantId.

```
data "azurerm_client_config" "current" {}
```

The next piece of code will create a resource group. There is no change here from the previous ACR deployment.

```
resource "azurerm_resource_group" "rg" {
  name      = "ApressAzureTerraformCH03"
  location = "australiasoutheast"
}
```

The code that follows will create an Azure Key Vault that we'll use to store the encryption key that will encrypt all the data in the container registry, including images.

Key Vault is configured with the following:

Enable Disk encryption
Enable Soft Delete
Enable purge protection
Use a Premium SKU

```
resource "azurerm_key_vault" "azvault" {
  name                          = "apresstfkeyvault"
  location                      = azurerm_resource_group.rg.location
  resource_group_name           = azurerm_resource_group.rg.name
  enabled_for_disk_encryption = true
  tenant_id                     = data.azurerm_client_config.current.
                                   tenant_id
  soft_delete_retention_days   = 7
  purge_protection_enabled     = true
  sku_name = "premium"

  access_policy {
    tenant_id = data.azurerm_client_config.current.tenant_id
    object_id = data.azurerm_client_config.current.object_id
    key_permissions = [
      "List",
      "Get",
      "Create",
      "Delete",
      "Get",
```

```
      "Purge",
      "Recover",
      "Update",
      "GetRotationPolicy",
      "SetRotationPolicy",
      "WrapKey",
      "UnwrapKey"

    ]

    secret_permissions = [
      "Get",
      "List",
      "Set"
    ]

    storage_permissions = [
      "Get",
      "List",
      "Set"
    ]
  }
}

data "azuread_service_principal" "serviceprincipal" {
  display_name = "acr-admin"
}
```

Next, we'll create a Key Vault access policy, which is an access policy control specifying what kind of permissions each Azure AD identity has access to in the Key Vault. In our case, we'll give a service principal account access to the vault with the permissions listed under key_permissions.

```
resource "azurerm_key_vault_access_policy" "example-principal" {
  key_vault_id = azurerm_key_vault.azvault.id
  tenant_id    = data.azurerm_client_config.current.tenant_id
  object_id    = data.azuread_service_principal.serviceprincipal.object_id
```

```
  key_permissions = [
    "List",
      "Get",
      "Create",
      "Delete",
      "Get",
      "Purge",
      "Recover",
      "Update",
      "GetRotationPolicy",
      "SetRotationPolicy",
      "WrapKey",
      "UnwrapKey"
  ]
}
```

The code that follows will read the name of the Azure Key Vault we created, as we'll need to use it soon.

```
data "azurerm_key_vault" "azvault" {
  name                 = azurerm_key_vault.azvault.name
  resource_group_name = azurerm_resource_group.rg.name

}
```

This next code block will create an Azure Key Vault key that we'll use to encrypt the data. The code has key configuration items like type and size. We're also defining what kind of operations are allowed with the key and rotation policy.

```
resource "azurerm_key_vault_key" "acrkey" {
  name         = "acraccess"
  key_vault_id = azurerm_key_vault.azvault.id
  key_type     = "RSA"
  key_size     = 2048

  key_opts = [
    "decrypt",
    "encrypt",
    "sign",
```

```
      "unwrapKey",
      "verify",
      "wrapKey",
      "unwrapKey"
  ]

  rotation_policy {
    automatic {
      time_before_expiry = "P30D"
    }

    expire_after          = "P90D"
    notify_before_expiry = "P29D"
  }
}
```

The following data source code block will read the name of the next key we created and stores it, as we will also use this one soon.

```
data "azurerm_key_vault_key" "readkey" {
  name         = azurerm_key_vault_key.acrkey.name
  key_vault_id = data.azurerm_key_vault.azvault.id
}
```

And in the next piece of code, we'll create a user-assigned identity that we'll use to manage ACR encryption and interaction with Azure Key Vault. The username is acr-admin.

```
resource "azurerm_user_assigned_identity" "identity" {
  resource_group_name = azurerm_resource_group.rg.name
  location             = azurerm_resource_group.rg.location
  name = "acr-admin"
}
```

The final block of code that follows will create an ACR with these features:

- managed identity enabled

- use of a premium SKU

- encryption enabled

- access granted to the managed identity account we created

```
resource "azurerm_container_registry" "acr" {
  name                = "apresstfacr"
  resource_group_name = azurerm_resource_group.rg.name
  location            = azurerm_resource_group.rg.location
  sku                 = "Premium"
  admin_enabled       = true

  tags = {
    environment = "dev"
  }

  identity {
    type = "UserAssigned"
    identity_ids = [
      azurerm_user_assigned_identity.identity.id

    ]
  }

  encryption {
      enabled             = true
      key_vault_key_id    = data.azurerm_key_vault_key.readkey.id
      identity_client_id  = azurerm_user_assigned_identity.identity.
      client_id
  }

}
```

The full code follows. It is important that you go over the code to understand how the configuration is done. An important thing to note is that Terraform decides how to deploy resources and determines the order of deployment without looking at the order the code is written in.

```
data "azurerm_client_config" "current" {}

resource "azurerm_resource_group" "rg" {
  name     = "ApressAzureTerraformCH03"
  location = "australiasoutheast"
}
```

```
resource "azurerm_key_vault" "azvault" {
  name                       = "apresstfkeyvault"
  location                   = azurerm_resource_group.rg.location
  resource_group_name        = azurerm_resource_group.rg.name
  enabled_for_disk_encryption = true
  tenant_id                  = data.azurerm_client_config.current.
                               tenant_id
  soft_delete_retention_days = 7
  purge_protection_enabled   = true
  sku_name = "premium"

  access_policy {
    tenant_id = data.azurerm_client_config.current.tenant_id
    object_id = data.azurerm_client_config.current.object_id

    key_permissions = [
      "List",
      "Get",
      "Create",
      "Delete",
      "Get",
      "Purge",
      "Recover",
      "Update",
      "GetRotationPolicy",
      "SetRotationPolicy",
      "WrapKey",
      "UnwrapKey"

    ]

    secret_permissions = [
      "Get",
      "List",
      "Set"
    ]
```

```
    storage_permissions = [
      "Get",
      "List",
      "Set"
    ]
  }
}

data "azuread_service_principal" "serviceprincipal" {
  display_name = "acr-admin"
}

resource "azurerm_key_vault_access_policy" "example-principal" {
  key_vault_id = azurerm_key_vault.azvault.id
  tenant_id    = data.azurerm_client_config.current.tenant_id
  object_id    = data.azuread_service_principal.serviceprincipal.object_id

  key_permissions = [
    "List",
      "Get",
      "Create",
      "Delete",
      "Get",
      "Purge",
      "Recover",
      "Update",
      "GetRotationPolicy",
      "SetRotationPolicy",
      "WrapKey",
      "UnwrapKey"
  ]
}

data "azurerm_key_vault" "azvault" {
  name                = azurerm_key_vault.azvault.name
  resource_group_name = azurerm_resource_group.rg.name

}
```

```
resource "azurerm_key_vault_key" "acrkey" {
  name          = "acraccess"
  key_vault_id = azurerm_key_vault.azvault.id
  key_type      = "RSA"
  key_size      = 2048

  key_opts = [
    "decrypt",
    "encrypt",
    "sign",
    "unwrapKey",
    "verify",
    "wrapKey",
    "unwrapKey"
  ]

  rotation_policy {
    automatic {
      time_before_expiry = "P30D"
    }

    expire_after         = "P90D"
    notify_before_expiry = "P29D"
  }
}

data "azurerm_key_vault_key" "readkey" {
  name          = azurerm_key_vault_key.acrkey.name
  key_vault_id = data.azurerm_key_vault.azvault.id
}

resource "azurerm_user_assigned_identity" "identity" {
  resource_group_name = azurerm_resource_group.rg.name
  location             = azurerm_resource_group.rg.location
  name = "acr-admin"
}
```

```
resource "azurerm_container_registry" "acr" {
  name                 = "apresstfacr"
  resource_group_name = azurerm_resource_group.rg.name
  location             = azurerm_resource_group.rg.location
  sku                  = "Premium"
  admin_enabled        = true

  tags = {
    environment = "dev"
  }

  identity {
    type = "UserAssigned"
    identity_ids = [
      azurerm_user_assigned_identity.identity.id

    ]
  }

  encryption {
      enabled             = true
      key_vault_key_id    = data.azurerm_key_vault_key.readkey.id
      identity_client_id = azurerm_user_assigned_identity.identity.
                           client_id
  }

}
```

Now, if you open the Azure portal, go to the newly deployed ACR, and click "Encryption," you'll see that encryption has been enabled using the identity we set in the code, as shown in Figure 3-1.

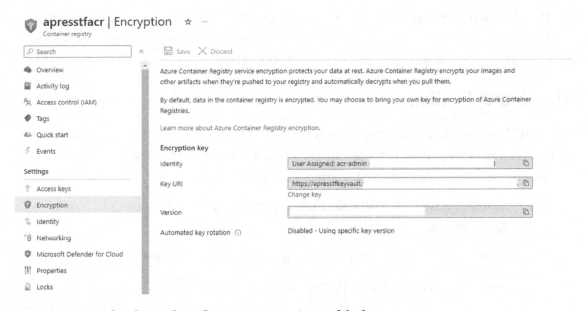

Figure 3-1. *Checking that the encryption is enabled*

Another thing that can be configured is the removal of public access to our ACR, so that it is only available to internal Azure networks, as shown in Figure 3-2.

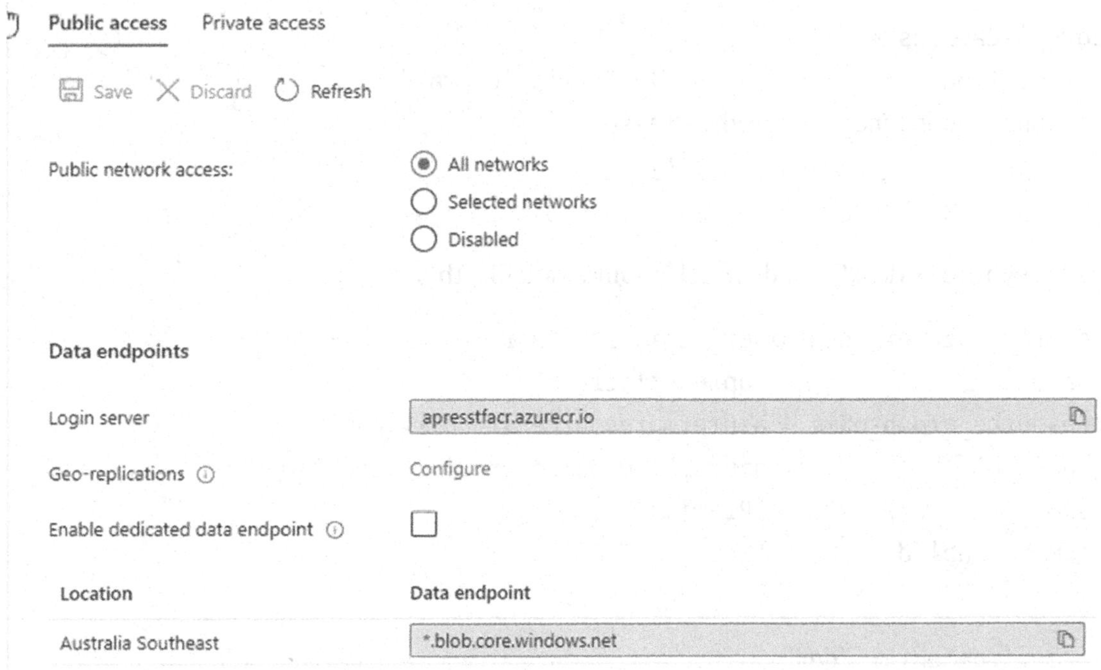

Figure 3-2. *Removing public access to ACR*

If you click the "Private Access" tab shown in Figure 3-2, you'll see that we can also configure ACR to have private access. After enabling private access to an ACR endpoint, ACR will accept traffic from private virtual networks only.

ACR Georeplication

Azure ACR allows us to optimize the performance of our container registry by enabling georeplication, so that it serves multiple regions using a single ACR registry.

The main benefits of using ACR georeplication are:

- an improvement of the performance and reliability of image deployments

- a reduction of the cost of data transfer across Azure regions

- being able to use a single ACR registry

- the ACR registry's resilience, essential in case of an outage in an Azure region

If needed, we can enable georeplication with Terraform by adding the following code block to the Key Vault code block:

```
georeplications {
    location                 = "Australia Central"
    zone_redundancy_enabled = false
    tags                     = {}
}
```

The entire code ACR code block should look like this:

```
resource "azurerm_container_registry" "acr" {
  name                = "apresstfacr"
  resource_group_name = azurerm_resource_group.rg.name
  location            = azurerm_resource_group.rg.location
  sku                 = "Premium"
  admin_enabled       = true

  tags = {
    environment = "dev"
  }
```

```
identity {
  type = "UserAssigned"
  identity_ids = [
    azurerm_user_assigned_identity.identity.id
  ]
}

encryption {
  enabled          = true
  key_vault_key_id   = data.azurerm_key_vault_key.readkey.id
  identity_client_id = azurerm_user_assigned_identity.identity.
  client_id
}

georeplications {
  location                = "Australia Central"
  zone_redundancy_enabled = false
  tags                    = {}
}

}
```

Once the replication is enabled, you can check the status from the ACR page in the Azure portal under "Georeplication," as shown in Figure 3-3. The two locations that form the Georeplications are shown under the Name header.

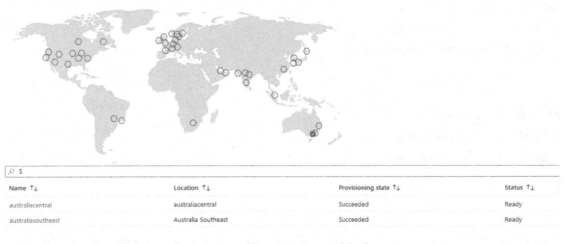

Name ↑↓	Location ↑↓	Provisioning state ↑↓	Status ↑↓
australiacentral	australiacentral	Succeeded	Ready
australiasoutheast	Australia Southeast	Succeeded	Ready

Figure 3-3. *Confirming that georeplication is enabled*

Using ACR with Azure Web App for Containers

Before we finish this chapter, I want to show you how we can use an Azure Container Registry in conjunction with Web App for Containers to pull images from a private registry. When we deployed Web App for Containers in Chapter 2, we used the Docker hub public registry, and we didn't need to provide any authentication details.

Now that we have a secure and private ACR up and running, we can use it with Web App for Containers and pull images directly from it.

In the next subsection, we'll learn about something new: Terraform variables that allow us to store the details of our ACR without having to hard-code directly in the Terraform configuration files.

Note   The code is available in the book repository under "Chapter02 -> WebappACR."

Using a Terraform Variables File

Terraform variables allow us to store variables like server names, usernames, and other details in a variable file and reference the variable during runtime.

In our case, we're going to use a variable file to store the details of our ACR. The configuration of the variable follows. The file is called `variables.tf`; you can name it anything you like, as Terraform doesn't care about the name of the file used.

```
variable "acr_image" {
  type    = string
  default = "ch03/image01:v1"

}

variable "acruser" {
  type    = string
  default = "apresstfacr"

}
```

```
variable "acr_server" {
  type       = string
  default = "https://apresstfacr.azurecr.io"

}

variable "acr_password" {
  type        = string

}
```

In the previous file, we have declared four variables, which we populated with default values. The last variable is the password for the ACR username, which we aren't going to save to the variable file. We'll pass the password as a parameter using the command line, as you will soon see.

Configuring Azure Web App with ACR

The configuration for Web App for Containers is the same as the one we used in Chapter 2. The only changes are in the Web App configuration section as follow:

```
docker_image_name      = var.acr_image
docker_registry_url = var.acr_server
docker_registry_username =  var.acruser
docker_registry_password = var.acr_password
```

As you can see, we are referencing the variables and not the actual values of the registry. To reference a variable, we use:

```
var.varname
```

The entire configuration for Web Apps for Containers with ACR registry is.

```
resource "azurerm_resource_group" "rg" {
  name      = "ApressAzureTerraformCH02"
  location = "Australia Southeast"
}
```

```
resource "random_integer" "random" {
  min = 1
  max = 20
}

resource "azurerm_service_plan" "appservice" {
  name                = "Linux"
  resource_group_name = azurerm_resource_group.rg.name
  location            = azurerm_resource_group.rg.location
  os_type             = "Linux"
  sku_name            = "S2"
}

resource "azurerm_linux_web_app" "webapp" {
  name                = "ApressTFWebApp${random_integer.random.result}"
  resource_group_name = azurerm_resource_group.rg.name
  location            = azurerm_resource_group.rg.location
  service_plan_id     = azurerm_service_plan.appservice.id

  https_only = "true"

site_config {
    always_on          = "true"
    minimum_tls_version = "1.1"
    application_stack {
      docker_image_name      = var.acr_image
      docker_registry_url = var.acr_server
      docker_registry_username =  var.acruser
      docker_registry_password = var.acr_password
    }

    ip_restriction {   # Use only if needed
      ip_address = "10.0.0.0/24"
      action      = "Allow"
    }

}
```

```
app_settings = {
    "DOCKER_ENABLE_CI" = "true"
}
}
```

Passing Variables Using "Terraform Apply"

As mentioned previously, we're not going to type the password of the ACR username in the variables file. We'll instead pass the password using the following command:

```
-var=varbame=varvalue
```

The following `Terraform apply` command will deploy the code and pass the password to Azure:

```
terraform apply -var="acrpassword= ACR PASSWORD"
```

Checking the Logs

Once Terraform has finished deploying the code, we can check if the web app managed to access the image using the deployment logs by doing the following:

1. To access the deployment logs, open the Azure portal and click on the web App we just deployed.

2. Click the "Deployment Center."

3. Click the "Logs" tab.

The logs are shown in the following:

```
INFO - Pulling image: apresstfacr.azurecr.io/ch03/image01:v1
INFO - v1 Pulling from ch03/image01
INFO - 1b930d010525 Pulling fs layer
INFO - 1b930d010525 Downloading 977B / 977B
INFO - 1b930d010525 Verifying Checksum
INFO - 1b930d010525 Download complete
INFO - 1b930d010525 Extracting 977B / 977B
INFO - 1b930d010525 Extracting 977B / 977B
```

```
INFO - 1b930d010525 Pull complete
INFO - Digest: sha256:92c7f9c92844bbbb5d0a101b22f7c2a7949e40f8ea90c8b3
       bc396879d95e899a
INFO - Status: Downloaded newer image for apresstfacr.azurecr.io/ch03/
       image01:v1
Pull Image successful, Time taken: 0 Minutes and 1 Seconds
```

Summary

In this chapter, we learned how to create an ACR registry with basic configuration as well as with advanced security features. The last part of the chapter was focused on the integration of ACR with Azure Web App for Containers.

## CHAPTER 4

Azure Container Instances

Introduction

In this chapter, we're going to explore and containers and learn how to deploy them to the Azure Container Instances (ACI) service using Terraform infrastructure provisioning. Azure ACI is a serverless container service that removes the underlying infrastructure and focuses on the deployment of containers. With ACI, developers and engineers can deploy applications without worrying about managing virtual machines and related services.

Key Benefits of ACI

The key benefits of working with ACI can be summarized as follows:

- *Speed and simplicity*: ACI simplifies deployments by eliminating the need for complex infrastructure.

- *Lack of a server*: ACI is a native serverless service, and users are charged for consumed resources only.

- *Security*: ACI workloads are secure and isolated; all applications run in their own dedicated environment.

- *Scalability*: ACI has a built-in autoscaling capability, allowing applications to scale per predefined autoscaling rules.

- *Integration*: ACI is fully integrated with other Azure services like ACR, Azure Functions, and others.

© Shimon Ifrah 2024
S. Ifrah, *Getting Started with Containers in Azure*, https://doi.org/10.1007/978-1-4842-9972-2_4

Use Cases

ACI's main use cases include the following scenarios:

- the development and testing of applications
- the deployment and architecture of microservices
- scaling and cost control
- running lightweight scheduled tasks

Deploying Azure Container Instances

To get started with ACI, we'll begin by deploying an instance using Terraform. In the following deployment, we'll use a public image that will pull an image from the Docker Hub public registry and deploy it as a Linux-based container.

We need to use the `azurerm_container_group` resource to deploy an ACI instance, which can deploy a single container or group of containers. In our case, we'll deploy a single container that exposes port HTTP (80) to the Internet and make it accessible using a web browser.

The following code configures the ACI instance, and as you can see, we can configure the container resource allocation and distribute CPU and memory.

```
resource "azurerm_container_group" "acigroup" {
  name                = "ApressTerraform"
  location            = azurerm_resource_group.rg.location
  resource_group_name = azurerm_resource_group.rg.name
  ip_address_type     = "Public"
  dns_name_label      = "apressterraformbook"
  os_type             = "Linux"

  container {
    name   = "web-server"
    image  = "httpd:latest"
    cpu    = "2"
    memory = "4"
```

```
  ports {
    port     = 80
    protocol = "TCP"
  }
}

tags = {
  environment = "dev"
}
}
```

The other components that are available for configuration are the image name, DNS name, IP address type, and name of the container.

Full Code

To deploy the container, we'll use the following full configuration and deploy it to Azure. As a reminder, the steps to deploy the container are as follows:

1. Save the file as a `.tf`.

2. Run Terraform init.

3. Run Terraform plan.

4. Run Terraform apply.

```
resource "azurerm_resource_group" "rg" {
  name     = "ApressAzureTerraformCH04"
  location = "westus"
}

resource "azurerm_container_group" "acigroup" {
  name                = "ApressTerraform"
  location            = azurerm_resource_group.rg.location
  resource_group_name = azurerm_resource_group.rg.name
  ip_address_type     = "Public"
  dns_name_label      = "apressterraformbook"
  os_type             = "Linux"
```

```
  container {
    name    = "web-server"
    image   = "httpd:latest"
    cpu     = "2"
    memory  = "4"

    ports {
      port     = 80
      protocol = "TCP"
    }
  }

  tags = {
    environment = "dev"
  }
}
```

To check whether the deployment was successful, I created an output file called output.tf that outputs all the information about the ACI instance to the terminal. The output will display the following details:

- the fully qualified domain name (FQDN)

- the resource ID

- the public IP

- the availability zone

- tags

The output.tf configuration file looks like this:

```
data "azurerm_container_group" "acigroup" {
  name                = azurerm_container_group.acigroup.name
  resource_group_name = azurerm_resource_group.rg.name
}

output "fqdn" {
  value = azurerm_container_group.acigroup.fqdn
}
```

```
output "id" {
  value = azurerm_container_group.acigroup.id
}

output "ip_address" {
  value = data.azurerm_container_group.acigroup.ip_address
}

output "zones" {
  value = data.azurerm_container_group.acigroup.zones
}

output "tags" {
  value = data.azurerm_container_group.acigroup.tags
}
```

Please note that for us to output values that are not in the configuration, we have to call the data resource of the entire resource, which in our case is `azurerm_container_group`.

Deploying Multiple ACI Containers

In the previous example, we deployed a single Azure Container Instances container, but if you need to deploy multiple instances, you can simply add them to the code like this:

```
container {
    name   = "web-server"
    image  = "httpd:latest"
    cpu    = "2"
    memory = "4"

    ports {
      port     = 80
      protocol = "TCP"
    }
  }
```

```
container {
   name   = "web-server02"
   image  = "nginx:latest"
   cpu    = "2"
   memory = "4"

   ports {
      port     = 82
      protocol = "TCP"
   }
}
```

Using Azure Container Instances with Azure Container Registry

The next step in our ACI configuration is to use a container image from a private repository, and as we learned in Chapter 03, we can use Azure Container Registry (ACR) to host container images in a private and secure environment rather than using a public registry.

In the following configuration, we're going to use a variable file to apply a Docker image stored in ACR, similar to the one we used in Chapter 03 to configure Web App for Containers. The following variables.tf file is the same as the one I used in Chapter 03, but, in this case, I will populate the file with the details of my ACR.

What follows is the content of the variables.tf file. The only missing variable is the password variable, which I will pass to Azure using the command line. As a reminder, variables are passed like this:

```
terraform apply -var="acrpassword= ACR PASSWORD"
```

The "Variables.tf" File

The following variables file (variables.tf) helps us define variables in our configuration and avoid hard-coding resource names and values.

```
variable "acr_image" {
  type    = string
  default = "ch03/image01:v1"

}
```

```
variable "acruser" {
  type    = string
  default = "apresstfacr"

}

variable "acr_server" {
  type    = string
  default = "https://apresstfacr.azurecr.io"

}

variable "acr_password" {
  type    = string

}
```

To configure an ACI instance to use a Docker image, I have added the following code block to handle the ACR authentication:

```
image_registry_credential {
  server   = var.acr_server
  username = var.acruser
  password = var.acr_password
}
```

In the container details, I am using a variable to reference the container image address as shown in the following code block:

```
container {
  name   = "container"
  image  = var.acr_image
  cpu    = "2"
  memory = "2"

  ports {
    port     = 80
    protocol = "TCP"
  }
```

The "Main.tf" File

You can review and run the complete code after you deploy an Azure Container Registry. The following code creates a Linux ACI with two CPUs and open port 80 for incoming traffic from the internet.

```
resource "azurerm_resource_group" "rg" {
  name     = "ApressAzureTerraformCH04"
  location = "westus"
}

resource "azurerm_container_group" "acigroup" {
  name                = "ApressTerraform"
  location            = azurerm_resource_group.rg.location
  resource_group_name = azurerm_resource_group.rg.name
  ip_address_type     = "Public"
  dns_name_label      = "apressterraformbook"
  os_type             = "Linux"

   image_registry_credential {
    server   = var.acr_server
    username = var.acruser
    password = var.acr_password
  }

   container {
    name   = "container"
    image  = var.acr_image
    cpu    = "2"
    memory = "2"

    ports {
      port     = 80
      protocol = "TCP"
    }
  }

  tags = {
    environment = "dev"
  }
}
```

Applying the Code

To run the code, use the `Terraform apply` command and pass the ACR password variable via a command line like this one:

```
terraform apply -var="acrpassword=ACR PASSWORD"
```

Mounting a Data Volume to an ACI Container

In this section, we're going to deploy a new container instance and mount an Azure file share volume to it. By default, ACI containers don't have any data volumes attached to them and are stateless, which means that once the container is restarted or stopped, the state is lost.

To overcome this issue, data volumes are mounted in the form of Azure file shares in order to deploy ACI instances. Because the data is external and not part of the ACI instance, once the instance is stopped, the data remains unaffected by the state change.

Azure file shares are only supported with Linux containers; therefore, in the following configuration, we will use Linux.

To mount a data volume to our ACI instance, we'll add three configuration blocks that will do the following:

- create a storage account

- create a storage share

- mount a volume

Let's start by breaking the down the new code before deploying to Azure.

Storage Account

The following code block will create a standard-tier storage account and locally redundant storage (LRS) replication type. Just remember that the Azure storage account needs to be unique in the platform.

```
resource "azurerm_storage_account" "storageact" {
  name                    = "apresstfch04storage"
  resource_group_name     = azurerm_resource_group.rg.name
  location                = azurerm_resource_group.rg.location
```

```
account_tier            = "Standard"
account_replication_type = "LRS"
}
```

You can name the storage account with any unique name and change the storage tier as needed. Also note that we're using the same resource group and location, as there is no need to change them.

Azure File Share

In order for the container to access a data volume, we need to create one. By default, Azure storage accounts come without any shares, storage blobs, or other type of storage and just act as a logical unit for storage.

The following code will create a file share with a 50-GB storage quote, which can be changed later on if needed either by using Terraform, Azure portal, Azure CLI, or Azure PowerShell.

```
resource "azurerm_storage_share" "share" {
  name                 = "aci-apress-tf-share"
  storage_account_name = azurerm_storage_account.storageact.name
  quota                = 50
}
```

Mounting Data Volume to the Container

The last block of code will mount the data volume to our ACI container and set the following parameters:

- the name

- the mount path inside the container

- the share name of Azure File Share

```
volume {
        name       = "logs"
        mount_path = "/apress/logs"
        read_only  = false
        share_name = azurerm_storage_share.share.name
```

```
        storage_account_name = azurerm_storage_account.storageact.name
        storage_account_key  = azurerm_storage_account.storageact.
                                primary_access_key
    }
```

After those three code blocks are added to the configuration, all that remains is to deploy the code with Terraform applied.

The Complete Code

The complete code is:

```
data "azurerm_client_config" "current" {}

resource "azurerm_resource_group" "rg" {
  name     = "ApressAzureTerraformCH04"
  location = "westus"
}

resource "azurerm_storage_account" "storageact" {
  name                     = "apresstfch04storage"
  resource_group_name      = azurerm_resource_group.rg.name
  location                 = azurerm_resource_group.rg.location
  account_tier             = "Standard"
  account_replication_type = "LRS"
}

resource "azurerm_storage_share" "share" {
  name                 = "aci-apress-tf-share"
  storage_account_name = azurerm_storage_account.storageact.name
  quota                = 50
}

resource "azurerm_container_group" "acigroup" {
  name                = "ApressTerraform"
  location            = azurerm_resource_group.rg.location
  resource_group_name = azurerm_resource_group.rg.name
  ip_address_type     = "Public"
```

```
dns_name_label      = "apressterraformbook"
os_type             = "Linux"

container {
  name    = "web-server"
  image   = "httpd:latest"
  cpu     = "2"
  memory  = "4"

  ports {
    port     = 80
    protocol = "TCP"
  }

  volume {
      name       = "logs"
      mount_path = "/apress/logs"
      read_only  = false
      share_name = azurerm_storage_share.share.name

      storage_account_name = azurerm_storage_account.storageact.name
      storage_account_key  = azurerm_storage_account.storageact.
                               primary_access_key
  }

}

tags = {
  environment = "dev"
}
}
```

Managing Azure Container Instances

So far in the chapter, we have managed to do the following:

- create an ACI Container

- connect the Azure Container Registry to an ACI container

- mount a data volume using Azure File Share

With the previous configuration in place, we now need to introduce it to the Azure management and monitoring capabilities of container instances. To get started, we'll begin by connecting to a running container terminal to check if the volume we mounted exists.

Connecting to a Running ACI Container

To check whether the volume was mounted and the logs of the container, we can use the Azure management console or the Azure CLI. To connect to a terminal session of a deployed ACI container, we will log in to the Azure portal and open the deployed ACI group, as follows:

1. Locate the "Settings" section.

2. Click "Containers," as shown in Figure 4-1.

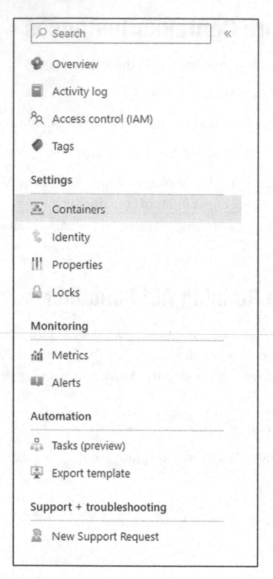

Figure 4-1. *Locating the "Containers" link*

You'll see the following information displayed in the "Containers" section of the page, as shown in Figure 4-2.

- the number of containers running

- the image name and version

- the state

- start time

On the lower section of the screen, there are four tabs:

- "Events"

- "Properties"

- "Logs"

- "Connect"

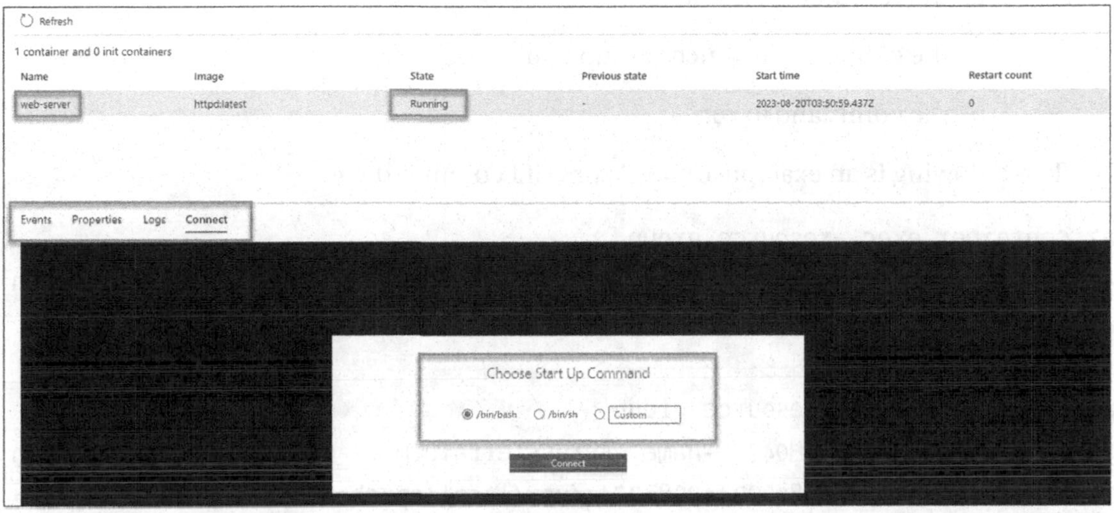

Figure 4-2. Containers page

Let's click the "Connect" tab, then select "/bin/bash" as the startup command and click "Connect."

Once connected, you'll be presented with a shell terminal where you can type any command that is available inside the installed shell. To check that the Apress directory was created, run the following command:

```
cd /apress
ls
```

The terminal output will be:

```
root@SandboxHost-638281002340986774:/usr/local/apache2# cd /apress/
root@SandboxHost-638281002340986774:/apress# ls
logs
root@SandboxHost-638281002340986774:/apress#
```

Using Azure CLI to Run Commands inside ACI

If you prefer to use Azure CLI to enter commands inside a running ACI container, this is possible as well. You can skip the portal and use the following steps:

1. Connect to Azure using: `az login`.

2. In a Linux container, run a command with:

   a. the resource group name

   b. the container instances group name

   c. the command to run

The following is an example of the Azure CLI command:

```
az container exec –resource-group
ApressAzureTerraformCH04  --name  ApressTerraform  --exec-command /bin/bash
```

The output will be:

```
az container exec --resource-group
ApressAzureTerraformCH04  --name  ApressTerraform  --exec-command /bin/bash
root@SandboxHost-638281002340986774:/usr/local/apache2# cd /apress/
root@SandboxHost-638281002340986774:/apress# ls
logs
root@SandboxHost-638281002340986774:/apress#
```

Viewing ACI Logs

We can view ACI logs using the "Logs" tab on the Containers page, as shown in Figure 4-3.

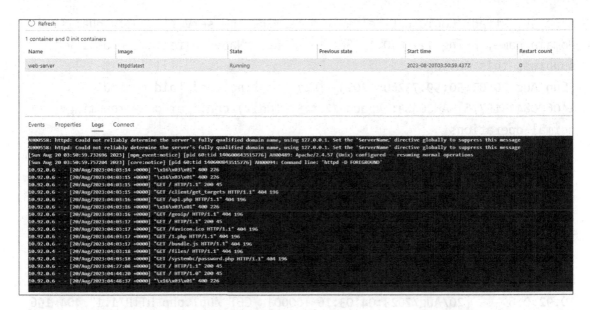

Figure 4-3. *Looking at ACI logs*

The logs are very detailed and will show any requests made to the container in real time.

Using Azure CLI to View Logs

If you prefer to use Azure CLI to view logs and automate some of the day-to-day tasks of checking the health of your container and logs, Azure CLI makes the process easy by offering the following command:

```
az container logs
```

In the case of our deployment, the command is:

```
az container logs --resource-group
ApressAzureTerraformCH04  --name  ApressTerraform
```

The output of the command will be:

```
AH00558: httpd: Could not reliably determine the server's fully qualified
domain name, using 127.0.0.1. Set the 'ServerName' directive globally to
suppress this message
```

AH00558: httpd: Could not reliably determine the server's fully qualified
domain name, using 127.0.0.1. Set the 'ServerName' directive globally to
suppress this message
[Sun Aug 20 03:50:59.732696 2023] [mpm_event:notice] [pid 60:tid
140600843515776] AH00489: Apache/2.4.57 (Unix) configured -- resuming
normal operations
[Sun Aug 20 03:50:59.757204 2023] [core:notice] [pid 60:tid
140600843515776] AH00094: Command line: 'httpd -D FOREGROUND'
10.92.0.6 - - [20/Aug/2023:04:03:14 +0000] "\x16\x03\x01" 400 226
10.92.0.6 - - [20/Aug/2023:04:03:15 +0000] "\x16\x03\x01" 400 226
10.92.0.6 - - [20/Aug/2023:04:03:15 +0000] "GET / HTTP/1.1" 200 45
10.92.0.6 - - [20/Aug/2023:04:03:15 +0000] "GET /client/get_targets
HTTP/1.1" 404 196
10.92.0.6 - - [20/Aug/2023:04:03:16 +0000] "GET /upl.php HTTP/1.1" 404 196
10.92.0.6 - - [20/Aug/2023:04:03:16 +0000] "\x16\x03\x01" 400 226
10.92.0.6 - - [20/Aug/2023:04:03:16 +0000] "GET /geoip/ HTTP/1.1" 404 196
10.92.0.6 - - [20/Aug/2023:04:03:17 +0000] "GET / HTTP/1.1" 200 45
10.92.0.6 - - [20/Aug/2023:04:03:17 +0000] "GET /favicon.ico
HTTP/1.1" 404 196
10.92.0.6 - - [20/Aug/2023:04:03:17 +0000] "GET /1.php HTTP/1.1" 404 196
10.92.0.6 - - [20/Aug/2023:04:03:17 +0000] "GET /bundle.js
HTTP/1.1" 404 196
10.92.0.4 - - [20/Aug/2023:04:03:18 +0000] "GET /files/ HTTP/1.1" 404 196
10.92.0.4 - - [20/Aug/2023:04:03:18 +0000] "GET /systembc/password.php
HTTP/1.1" 404 196
10.92.0.6 - - [20/Aug/2023:04:27:08 +0000] "GET / HTTP/1.1" 200 45
10.92.0.6 - - [20/Aug/2023:04:44:20 +0000] "GET / HTTP/1.0" 200 45
10.92.0.6 - - [20/Aug/2023:04:48:37 +0000] "\x16\x03\x01" 400 226

Viewing Diagnostic Information

We can also view a container's startup logs, which will help us troubleshoot deployment
and configuration issues. We do that by reviewing the STDOUT (standard output) ad
STDERR (standard error) streams of the console.

The command to do that is:

```
Az container attach
```

To view the streams log of our container, we need to run the following command:

```
az container attach --resource-group
ApressAzureTerraformCHO4  --name  ApressTerraform
```

This command will produce the output of the streams, which looks like:

```
Container 'web-server' is in state 'Running'...

Start streaming logs:
AHO0558: httpd: Could not reliably determine the server's fully qualified
domain name, using 127.0.0.1. Set the 'ServerName' directive globally to
suppress this message
AHO0558: httpd: Could not reliably determine the server's fully qualified
domain name, using 127.0.0.1. Set the 'ServerName' directive globally to
suppress this message
[Sun Aug 20 03:50:59.732696 2023] [mpm_event:notice] [pid 60:tid
140600843515776] AHO0489: Apache/2.4.57 (Unix) configured -- resuming
normal operations
[Sun Aug 20 03:50:59.757204 2023] [core:notice] [pid 60:tid
140600843515776] AHO0094: Command line: 'httpd -D FOREGROUND'
10.92.0.6 - - [20/Aug/2023:04:03:14 +0000] "\x16\x03\x01" 400 226
10.92.0.6 - - [20/Aug/2023:04:03:15 +0000] "\x16\x03\x01" 400 226
10.92.0.6 - - [20/Aug/2023:04:03:15 +0000] "GET / HTTP/1.1" 200 45
10.92.0.6 - - [20/Aug/2023:04:03:15 +0000] "GET /client/get_targets
HTTP/1.1" 404 196
10.92.0.6 - - [20/Aug/2023:04:03:16 +0000] "GET /upl.php HTTP/1.1" 404 196
10.92.0.6 - - [20/Aug/2023:04:03:16 +0000] "\x16\x03\x01" 400 226
10.92.0.6 - - [20/Aug/2023:04:03:16 +0000] "GET /geoip/ HTTP/1.1" 404 196
10.92.0.6 - - [20/Aug/2023:04:03:17 +0000] "GET / HTTP/1.1" 200 45
10.92.0.6 - - [20/Aug/2023:04:03:17 +0000] "GET /favicon.ico
HTTP/1.1" 404 196
10.92.0.6 - - [20/Aug/2023:04:03:17 +0000] "GET /1.php HTTP/1.1" 404 196
```

```
10.92.0.6 - - [20/Aug/2023:04:03:17 +0000] "GET /bundle.js
HTTP/1.1" 404 196
10.92.0.4 - - [20/Aug/2023:04:03:18 +0000] "GET /files/ HTTP/1.1" 404 196
10.92.0.4 - - [20/Aug/2023:04:03:18 +0000] "GET /systembc/password.php
HTTP/1.1" 404 196
10.92.0.6 - - [20/Aug/2023:04:27:08 +0000] "GET / HTTP/1.1" 200 45
10.92.0.6 - - [20/Aug/2023:04:44:20 +0000] "GET / HTTP/1.0" 200 45
10.92.0.6 - - [20/Aug/2023:04:48:37 +0000] "\x16\x03\x01" 400 226
```

Reviewing Diagnostic Events

To tap into the diagnostic event stream of our ACI container, we can use the following command:

```
az container show
```

In our case, the command will look like this:

```
az container show  --resource-group
ApressAzureTerraformCH04  --name  ApressTerraform
```

The output of the diagnostic command will show up in a JSON format like the following:

```
{
  "confidentialComputeProperties": null,
  "containers": [
    {
      "command": [],
      "environmentVariables": [],
      "image": "httpd:latest",
      "instanceView": {
        "currentState": {
          "detailStatus": "",
          "exitCode": null,
          "finishTime": null,
          "startTime": "2023-08-20T03:50:59.437000+00:00",
          "state": "Running"
        },
```

```
        "events": [],
        "previousState": null,
        "restartCount": 0
      },
      "livenessProbe": null,
      "name": "web-server",
      "ports": [
        {
          "port": 80,
          "protocol": "TCP"
        }
      ],
      "readinessProbe": null,
      "resources": {
        "limits": null,
        "requests": {
          "cpu": 2.0,
          "gpu": null,
          "memoryInGb": 4.0
        }
      },
      "securityContext": null,
      "volumeMounts": [
        {
          "mountPath": "/apress/logs",
          "name": "logs",
          "readOnly": false
        }
      ]
    }
  ],
  "diagnostics": null,
  "dnsConfig": null,
  "encryptionProperties": null,
  "extensions": null,
```

```
"id": "/subscriptions/SUBID/resourceGroups/ApressAzureTerraformCH04/
providers/Microsoft.ContainerInstance/containerGroups/ApressTerraform",
"identity": {
  "principalId": null,
  "tenantId": null,
  "type": "None",
  "userAssignedIdentities": null
},
"imageRegistryCredentials": null,
"initContainers": [],
"instanceView": {
  "events": [
    {
      "count": 1,
      "firstTimestamp": "2023-08-20T03:50:58.525000+00:00",
      "lastTimestamp": "2023-08-20T03:50:58.525000+00:00",
      "message": "Successfully mounted Azure File Volume.",
      "name": "SuccessfulMountAzureFileVolume",
      "type": "Normal"
    }
  ],
  "state": "Running"
},
"ipAddress": {
  "autoGeneratedDomainNameLabelScope": "Unsecure",
  "dnsNameLabel": "apressterraformbook",
  "fqdn": "apressterraformbook.westus.azurecontainer.io",
  "ip": "40.78.2.90",
  "ports": [
    {
      "port": 80,
      "protocol": "TCP"
    }
  ],
  "type": "Public"
},
```

```
"location": "westus",
"name": "ApressTerraform",
"osType": "Linux",
"priority": null,
"provisioningState": "Succeeded",
"resourceGroup": "ApressAzureTerraformCH04",
"restartPolicy": "Always",
"sku": "Standard",
"subnetIds": null,
"tags": {
  "environment": "dev"
},
"type": "Microsoft.ContainerInstance/containerGroups",
"volumes": [
  {
    "azureFile": {
      "readOnly": false,
      "shareName": "aci-apress-tf-share",
      "storageAccountKey": null,
      "storageAccountName": "apresstfch04storage"
    },
    "emptyDir": null,
    "gitRepo": null,
    "name": "logs",
    "secret": null
  }
],
"zones": null
}
```

The diagnostic information is important when trying to troubleshoot an issue with the container.

Enabling Advanced Log Collection

In the previous section, we looked at how to view logs on a running ACI deployment per group or container. The issue with this approach is that it doesn't scale well with multiple deployments or a large number of containers.

Because of this reason, it is better to centralize the collection of logs into central log storage and analyze the logs.

In the following configuration, we're going to enable Azure Log Analytics in our ACI deployment and configure ACI to send container logs to a Log Analytics collection, where we can view and analyze them.

Configuring Azure Log Analytics

To configure Log Analytics in our ACI group, we're going to add two configuration items to our last deployment without stopping the instances that are currently running. We'll add one code block that will create a Log Analytics workspace and a second configuration block to our ACI group with the details of the newly created Log Analytics.

The Log Analytics Resource Block

The first addition to our Terraform configuration will add a workspace, as follows. We can name the resource and set the SKU and retention period.

```
resource "azurerm_log_analytics_workspace" "log_analytics" {
  name                = "apresstfch04storagelogs"
  location            = azurerm_resource_group.rg.location
  resource_group_name = azurerm_resource_group.rg.name
  sku                 = "PerGB2018"
  retention_in_days   = 30
}
```

In the `azurerm_container_group`, we need to add a diagnostics code block to tell ACI to send all the logs to Log Analytics, where can review them and run reports against them.

The code to do so is:

```
diagnostics {
  log_analytics {
    workspace_id =  azurerm_log_analytics_workspace.log_analytics.
    workspace_id
    workspace_key = azurerm_log_analytics_workspace.log_analytics.
    primary_shared_key
  }
}
```

When you're ready, run the code to start the deployment.

Completing the Configuration Code

The complete Terraform configuration is:

```
data "azurerm_client_config" "current" {}

resource "azurerm_resource_group" "rg" {
  name     = "ApressAzureTerraformCH04"
  location = "westus"
}

resource "azurerm_log_analytics_workspace" "log_analytics" {
  name                = "apresstfch04storagelogs"
  location            = azurerm_resource_group.rg.location
  resource_group_name = azurerm_resource_group.rg.name
  sku                 = "PerGB2018"
  retention_in_days   = 30
}

resource "azurerm_storage_account" "storageact" {
  name                     = "apresstfch04storage"
  resource_group_name      = azurerm_resource_group.rg.name
  location                 = azurerm_resource_group.rg.location
  account_tier             = "Standard"
  account_replication_type = "LRS"
}
```

```
resource "azurerm_storage_share" "share" {
  name                 = "aci-apress-tf-share"
  storage_account_name = azurerm_storage_account.storageact.name
  quota                = 50
}

resource "azurerm_container_group" "acigroup" {
  name                = "ApressTerraform"
  location            = azurerm_resource_group.rg.location
  resource_group_name = azurerm_resource_group.rg.name
  ip_address_type     = "Public"
  dns_name_label      = "apressterraformbook"
  os_type             = "Linux"

  diagnostics {
    log_analytics {
      workspace_id =  azurerm_log_analytics_workspace.log_analytics.
      workspace_id
      workspace_key = azurerm_log_analytics_workspace.log_analytics.
      primary_shared_key
    }
  }

  container {
    name   = "web-server"
    image  = "httpd:latest"
    cpu    = "2"
    memory = "4"

    ports {
      port     = 80
      protocol = "TCP"
    }

    volume {
        name       = "logs"
        mount_path = "/apress/logs"
        read_only  = false
```

```
        share_name = azurerm_storage_share.share.name

        storage_account_name = azurerm_storage_account.storageact.name
        storage_account_key  = azurerm_storage_account.storageact.
        primary_access_key
    }
  }
  tags = {
    environment = "dev"
  }
}
```

Viewing the Logs

Once the deployment is complete, it's time to check if logs are being shipped to Log Analytics. To do so, first open the ACI deployment and restart the Container group. You can use the Azure portal to restart the group by clicking "Restart" on the "Overview" page of the Container group, as shown in Figure 4-4.

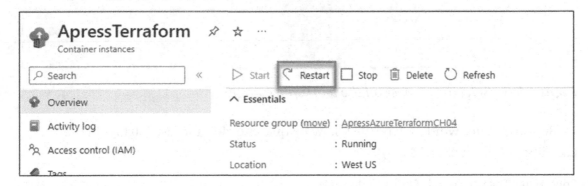

Figure 4-4. *Restarting ACI instances on the "Overview" page*

Once the restart is complete, you'll be able to see Log Analytics in action. In the Azure portal, search for Log Analytics workspaces.

The newly created workspace is shown in Figure 4-5.

Figure 4-5. *Log Analytics workspace*

On the workspace page, click "Logs," as shown in Figure 4-6.

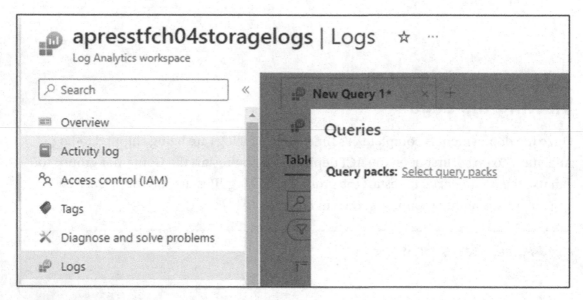

Figure 4-6. *Selecting "Logs" on the workspace page*

In the Queries window, type the following query to view the last 200 logs in the containers running in ACI.

```
ContainerInstanceLog_CL | limit 200
```

The results are shown in Figure 4-7.

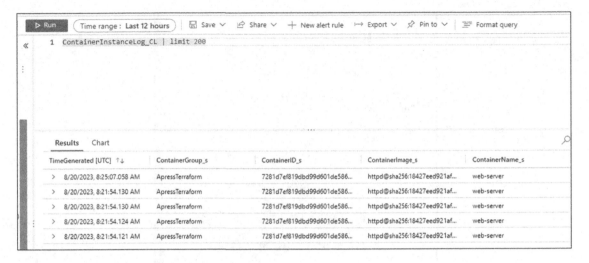

Figure 4-7. *Viewing the last 200 log entries*

To view the last 200 events, run the following query:

```
ContainerEvent_CL | limit 200
```

If you'd like to learn more about the Log Analytics log query, you can visit the log language page, Kusto Query Language (KQL) Overview used by Azure: `https://learn.microsoft.com/en-us/azure/data-explorer/kusto/query/`.

For ACI deployment, the main query source tables are:

- `ContainerInstanceLog_CL`

- `ContainerEvent_CL`

These tables contain information about logs and events generated by ACI containers. The log and event schemas are available for viewing on the Logs query page under "Custom Logs," as shown in Figure 4-8.

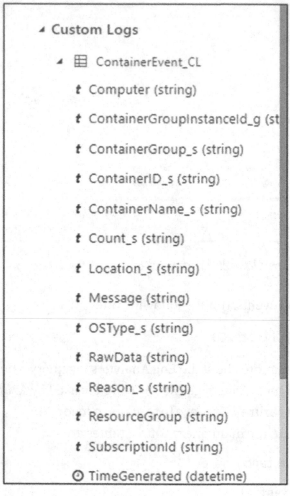

Figure 4-8. *Log Schema*

Stopping, Starting, and Restarting ACI Containers with Azure CLI

In the previous section, I asked you to restart your ACI deployment in order to generate events and logs in Log Analytics. We used the Azure portal to restart a running container.

In many scenarios, using the portal is not optimal and might not scale well in the many use cases where automation is used.

We can stop, start, and restart containers with Azure CLI by using the following Azure CLI commands.

Stopping the Container Group

To stop a running container, you can use this command: `Az container stop`.

In our case, the command will look like this:

```
az container stop --name ApressTerraform --resource-group
ApressAzureTerraformCH04 --verbose –debug
```

I've also added the verbose and debug switches to get more visibility into the stop process.

Starting the Container Group

To start a container, this is the command to use: `az container start`.

In our case, the command will look like this:

```
az container start --name ApressTerraform --resource-group
ApressAzureTerraformCH04 --verbose –debug
```

The output of the command will be:

```
\ Running ..
```

cli.azure.cli.core.sdk.policies: {"id":"/subscriptions/SUBID/
resourceGroups/ApressAzureTerraformCH04/providers/Microsoft.
ContainerInstance/containerGroups/ApressTerraform","status":"Succeeded
","startTime":"2023-08-20T09:13:01.6699127Z","properties":{"events":[{
"count":1,"firstTimestamp":"2023-08-20T08:21:33Z","lastTimestamp":"2023-
08-20T08:21:33Z","name":"Pulling","message":"pulling image \"httpd@sha25
6:18427eed921af003c951b5c97f0bde8a6df40cc7cb09b9739b9e35041a3c3acd\"","
type":"Normal"},{"count":1,"firstTimestamp":"2023-08-20T08:21:39Z","las
tTimestamp":"2023-08-20T08:21:39Z","name":"Pulled","message":"Successfu
lly pulled image \"httpd@sha256:18427eed921af003c951b5c97f0bde8a6df40cc
7cb09b9739b9e35041a3c3acd\"","type":"Normal"},{"count":2,"firstTimesta
mp":"2023-08-20T08:21:54Z","lastTimestamp":"2023-08-20T08:32:24Z","name":"S
tarted","message":"Started container","type":"Normal"},{"count":1,"firstTim
estamp":"2023-08-20T08:32:23Z","lastTimestamp":"2023-08-20T08:32:23Z","nam
e":"Killing","message":"Killing container with id 7281d7ef819dbd99d601de58
6032bfcedd0e8468b7bcdff1b0707e50067976f1.","type":"Normal"},{"count":1,"fi
```

117
```

rstTimestamp":"2023-08-20T09:13:06Z","lastTimestamp":"2023-08-20T09:13:06Z
","name":"Pulling","message":"pulling image \"httpd@sha256:18427eed921af00
3c951b5c97f0bde8a6df40cc7cb09b9739b9e35041a3c3acd\"","type":"Normal"},{"co
unt":1,"firstTimestamp":"2023-08-20T09:13:13Z","lastTimestamp":"2023-08-2
0T09:13:13Z","name":"Pulled","message":"Successfully pulled image \"httpd@
sha256:18427eed921af003c951b5c97f0bde8a6df40cc7cb09b9739b9e35041a3c3acd\"",
"type":"Normal"},{"count":1,"firstTimestamp":"2023-08-20T09:13:30Z","lastTi
mestamp":"2023-08-20T09:13:30Z","name":"Started","message":"Started contain
er","type":"Normal"},{"count":1,"firstTimestamp":"2023-08-20T08:21:53.547Z"
,"lastTimestamp":"2023-08-20T08:21:53.547Z","name":"SuccessfulMountAzureFil
eVolume","message":"Successfully mounted Azure File Volume.","type":"Normal
"},{"count":1,"firstTimestamp":"2023-08-20T09:13:29.124Z","lastTimestamp":"
2023-08-20T09:13:29.124Z","name":"SuccessfulMountAzureFileVolume","message"
:"Successfully mounted Azure File Volume.","type":"Normal"}]}}

```
cli.knack.cli: Event: CommandInvoker.OnTransformResult [<function _
resource_group_transform at 0x7f1c957f6cb0>, <function _x509_from_base64_
to_hex_transform at 0x7f1c957f6d40>]
cli.knack.cli: Event: CommandInvoker.OnFilterResult []
cli.knack.cli: Event: Cli.SuccessfulExecute []
cli.knack.cli: Event: Cli.PostExecute [<function AzCliLogging.deinit_cmd_
metadata_logging at 0x7f1c957af010>]
```

Restarting the Container Group

To restart a running container group, the following command can be used:

```
az container restart   --no-wait.
```

In our case, the full command will look like this:

```
az container restart --name ApressTerraform --resource-group
ApressAzureTerraformCH04 --verbose --debug --no-wait
```

Liveness and Readiness Probes

In the last section of this book, I will cover how to add liveness and readiness probes to an ACI container group to detect if the actual container has an issue and only accepts the request when the container is ready.

Liveness Probes

A liveness probe runs regular checks that diagnose the health of the container instance. It automatically triggers a restart if it detects that the container isn't responding to the checks.

Liveness probes are handy because they help us detect if the container needs a restart. We configure liveness probs by specifying a path, port, or command that ACI will run periodically.

If the command is successful, the container is marked as healthy and no action is taken. If the check fails a few times, the container is marked as unhealthy and restarted automatically.

Readiness Probe

A readiness probe checks if the application is ready to accept incoming traffic after it completes a restart process. The checking mechanism is similar to that of the liveness probe and will result in stopping traffic from being directed into the container.

To configure these two probes, let's add the following configuration blocks and a single command to the container configuration block:

```
commands = ["/bin/sh","-c","sleep 30","touch /tmp/healthy; sleep 30; rm -rf
/tmp/healthy; sleep 600"]

    readiness_probe {
      exec = ["cat","/tmp/healthy"]
      initial_delay_seconds = 2
      period_seconds = 60
      failure_threshold = 3
      success_threshold = 1
      timeout_seconds = 40
    }
```

```
liveness_probe {
  exec = ["cat","/tmp/healthy"]
  initial_delay_seconds = 2
  period_seconds = 60
  failure_threshold = 3
  success_threshold = 1
  timeout_seconds = 40

}
```

Summary

In this chapter, we learned about deploying Azure Container Instances and how to do the following:

- integrate an ACI deployment with Azure Container Registry

- deploy multiple containers

- mount data volume to an ACI deployment

- view diagnostic information

- enable advanced log collection

- configure probes

CHAPTER 5

Azure Kubernetes Service

Introduction

In this chapter, we'll take a deep dive into the Microsoft Azure Kubernetes Service (AKS) and learn how to deploy and manage containerized applications with the service. So far, we've covered the two main container services on Azure. Now, we'll move to the third service, Kubernetes, which is considered an enterprise-ready solution.

About Kubernetes

Kubernetes is an orchestration and automation container management system developed by Google that was turned into an open-source platform in 2014. Kubernetes is so powerful that it is used by Google to run over one billion containers and power many of its cloud services.

The scalability of Kubernetes is almost unlimited, which gives enterprises the ability to scale up or down during a short time. It is currently considered the standard tool for container management and automation in small and large organizations and has a market share of almost 80 percent and growing.

There is no doubt that Kubernetes is the current go-to tool for orchestration and automation.

Kubernetes Components

In this section, I will go over each of the components that make up Kubernetes. Once we move on to working with AKS, we will use the knowledge of these components to understand the service better.

© Shimon Ifrah 2023
S. Ifrah, *Getting Started with Containers in Azure*, https://doi.org/10.1007/978-1-4842-9972-2_5

Kubernetes is made up of the following three main components, each one consisting of three subcomponents.

Kubernetes Master

Kubernetes Master is the most important component in Kubernetes, and as the name implies, it is the master node, also known as the "control plane," from which calculations and automation are controlled.

The Kubernetes Master is made up of five components:

- *Kube-apiserver*: This the API server that exposes all the APIs of Kubernetes to other components.

- *Etcd*: This is the key-value storage component that stores the cluster data.

- *Kube-scheduler*: The scheduler makes sure new pods are matched with a node.

- *Kube controller-manager*: The controller-manager is responsible for managing nodes, replicating between the nodes and the master, endpoints, and tokens.

- *Cloud-controller manager*: This is a new component that was released with version 1.6 of Kubernetes. It helps cloud providers control updates and releases of their Kubernetes deployments.

Each controller is a separate logical component. However, they are managed as a single process on the master.

Kubernetes Nodes

In Kubernetes, the nodes are the actual servers that run the containers, also known as pods.

The nodes are the computing units that perform the heavy lifting of deploying pods, volumes, and networking.

The nodes have three components:

- *The kubelet*: This agent service runs on each node and ensures that pods are running as planned.

- *The kube proxy*: This network component makes sure services are operated according to the network policies and rules set by the master component.

- *The container runtime*: This is the runtime container software that runs the containers, and in our case, this is where Docker is running.

Kubernetes Add-Ons

Add-ons are optional features that can be added to the Kubernetes cluster. The following add-ons are just a few of the many available:

- *DNS*: This is a DNS service that serves DNS name resolution for Kubernetes; by default, all Kubernetes components are used.

- *Web UI (dashboard)*: Web UI is a browser-based interface for Kubernetes management that allows users to perform administrative tasks using a web-based interface.

- *Container resource monitor*: This monitor logs metrics about running containers inside the cluster.

- *Cluster-level logging*: The logging records information about our Kubernetes cluster.

Now that we have some background information about Kubernetes, let's move to the next section, which will cover the Azure implementation of Kubernetes.

Getting Started with AKS

Before we get started with AKS and create our first cluster, it's important that we understand the platform's management domain. In the previous section, we learned about all the Kubernetes components and what each one does.

In AKS, Microsoft Azure is responsible for managing the master components. The master components are beyond our reach, with users not being granted access to them. This fact takes [^away] the complexity of managing Kubernetes and leaves [^it up to us to only manage the nodes].

Our control of AKS involves managing the Kubernetes nodes with minimal administrative tasks necessary, like scaling and updating them. In this section, we'll go over the deployment process of AKS using Terraform and Azure CLI.

Deploying the AKS Cluster

To get started with AKS, let's deploy a single-node cluster using the following Terraform configuration. At a minimum, an AKS cluster requires a single-node cluster running Linux. Windows nodes are also available, but they are outside of the scope of this book.

```
resource "azurerm_resource_group" "rg" {
  name     = "ApressAzureTerraformCH05"
  location = "australia southeast"
}

resource "azurerm_kubernetes_cluster" "akscluster" {
  name                = "aks"
  location            = azurerm_resource_group.rg.location
  resource_group_name = azurerm_resource_group.rg.name
  dns_prefix          = "aks"

  default_node_pool {
    name       = "default"
    node_count = var.node_count
    vm_size    = "Standard_D2_v2"
  }

  identity {
    type = "SystemAssigned"
  }

  tags = {
    Environment = "DEV"
  }
}
```

To deploy the cluster, we'll use the code in this book's repository and run the following Terraform commands:

- Terraform init

- Terraform plan

- Terraform apply

After running Terraform, you'll need to apply the commands, review the output, and then make sure the cluster was deployed successfully. In the next section, we'll learn how to connect to an AKS cluster using Azure CLI and deploy containerized applications to the cluster.

Connecting to AKS Using the Azure Command-Line Interface

Before we get started deploying a cluster, it might be a good idea to read an overview of the process on the Microsoft Ignite site: https://learn.microsoft.com/en-us/azure/aks/learn/quick-kubernetes-deploy-cli.

To connect to a running AKS cluster on Azure, we use the Kubernetes command-line client known as kubectl. To get the client installed, we'll use the Azure CLI command az aks install-cli.

Once the installation is complete, we can configure the CLI to connect to the cluster by first retrieving the credentials using the following command:

az aks get-credentials --resource-group   RGNAME –name CLUSTERNAME

If you're following the code of this book, the command will look like this:

az aks get-credentials --resource-group ApressAzureTerraformCH05 --name AKS

At this stage, we can go ahead and use the kubectl command to check the status of the nodes in our cluster. In our case, the following command will show one node:

kubectl get nodes

The output of the command should look like this:

```
NAME                            STATUS   ROLES   AGE   VERSION
aks-default-13103899-vmss000000  Ready    agent   11m   v1.26.6
```

Deploying an Application to the AKS Cluster

Deploying applications to an AKS cluster requires us to use the kubectl command-line utility with a YAML configuration file that describes the deployment of the application.

Using the code in the next section, we'll deploy the nginx web server application using a public Docker image from the Docker Hub repository. To deploy an application to our AKS cluster, follow these steps:

- Create a file called deployment.yaml.

- Use kubectl to deploy the application.

- Validate the deployment using kubectl.

The "Deployment.yaml" File

We can use the following YAML file to deploy the nginx web server application to our AKS cluster by saving the file in the same directory as the one where we run the Terraform deployment:

```
apiVersion: apps/v1
kind: Deployment
metadata:
  name: web-server
spec:
  replicas: 1
  selector:
    matchLabels:
      app: web-server
  template:
    metadata:
      labels:
        app: web-server
    spec:
      nodeSelector:
        "kubernetes.io/os": linux
      containers:
      - name: web-server
        image: nginx:latest
```

```
      resources:
        requests:
          cpu: 100m
          memory: 128Mi
        limits:
          cpu: 250m
          memory: 256Mi
      ports:
      - containerPort: 80
        name: redis
---
apiVersion: v1
kind: Service
metadata:
  name: web-server
spec:
  type: LoadBalancer
  ports:
  - port: 80
  selector:
    app: web-server
```

If you look at the previous configuration file, you'll see that I'm using a separator (---) to divide the deployment and the service. Kubernetes allows me to create a separate file for the service.

We set the kind of deployment in the following configuration file. In this example, the kind is Deployment.

```
apiVersion: apps/v1
kind: Deployment
metadata:
  name: web-server
```

Now, run the following command to deploy the application:

```
kubectl apply -f deployment.yaml
```

The output of the command should look like this:

```
deployment.apps/web-server created
service/web-server created
```

Checking the Deployment Status

To check the deployment status of the application, we can use the following command:

```
kubectl get service web-server -watch
```

The command output should look like this:

```
NAME          TYPE           CLUSTER-IP      EXTERNAL-IP     PORT(S)        AGE
web-server    LoadBalancer   10.0.92.177     20.198.195.40   80:30821/TCP   10s
```

We can copy the IP address in the EXTERNAL-IP field to check if the application is working. If you open a web browser and paste the external IP address in the address bar, you'll come the home page of the nginx web server interface shown in Figure 5-1.

Figure 5-1. *Nginx home page*

Deleting the Deployment

Once you're happy with the results, you can delete the deployment from the AKS cluster by using the following command:

```
kubectl delete -f deployment.yaml
```

Scaling the Application

In Kubernetes, the process of scaling applications is simple and straightforward because the containers are stateless and don't store any data except configuration items.

If you look at our `deployment.yaml` configuration file, you'll notice the `replicas` item, which is set to 1 pod. We can easily change the replica value, create more pods, and scale applications to allow more capacity.

We can scale applications by either changing the value of the replicas in the configuration file or running the following command:

```
kubectl scale --replicas=3 deployment/web-server
```

Enabling Autoscaling

Another helpful feature of AKS is the ability to configure the deployment to autoscale automatically based on usage. For example, autoscaling can scale the pods in case the CPU level increases to 60 percent.

Autoscaling can be configured using the `kubectl` command or a configuration file.

When using `kubectl`, the following command will automatically scale the deployment if the CPU usage increases to 60 percent. The minimum number of pods in the deployment is set to 2 and the maximum to 5.

```
kubectl autoscale deployment azure-vote-front --cpu-percent=60
--min=2--max=5
```

Just keep in mind that in order for autoscaling to work, a CPU limit must be defined for the containers and pods in the deployment.

To use the configuration file for autoscaling, we can use the following `deployment.yaml` file. We will deploy this file after we deploy the application and service.

```
apiVersion: autoscaling/v1
kind: HorizontalPodAutoscaler
metadata:
  name: web-app-ha
spec:
  maxReplicas: 5
  minReplicas: 2
  scaleTargetRef:
```

```
  apiVersion: apps/v1
  kind: Deployment
  name: web-server
targetCPUUtilizationPercentage: 60
```

To check if autoscaling is working and its status, we can use the following command:

```
kubectl get hpa
```

The output should look like this:

NAME	REFERENCE	TARGETS	MINPODS	MAXPODS	REPLICAS	AGE
web-app-ha	Deployment/web-server	1%/60%	2	5	2	2m40s

Connecting the AKS Cluster to the Azure Container Registry

Now that we know how to deploy an AKS cluster to Microsoft Azure using Terraform, we can go on to the next step and learn how to integrate AKS with the Azure Container Registry, reviewed in Chapter 3.

In the following configuration, we'll deploy an AKS cluster and ACR registry togther and establish a connection between them using a system-assigned identity.

Note   The code for this deployment is available in the Chapter 5 repository.

The following code will deploy both AKS and an ACR registry. The code is the same as that for the previous AKS deployment except for the following two new configuration blocks:

- *ACR configuration block*: Deploys an ACR registry

    ```
    resource "azurerm_container_registry" "acr" {
      name                = "apresstfacr"
      resource_group_name = azurerm_resource_group.rg.name
      location            = azurerm_resource_group.rg.location
      sku                 = "Premium"
      admin_enabled       = true
    }
    ```

- *Azure role assignment configuration block*: Establishes an authentication mechanism with AKS

```
resource "azurerm_role_assignment" "role" {
  principal_id                      = azurerm_kubernetes_cluster.
  akscluster.kubelet_identity[0].object_id
  role_definition_name      = "AcrPull"
  scope                              = azurerm_container_
  registry.acr.id
  skip_service_principal_aad_check = true
}
```

The full code follows:

```
resource "azurerm_resource_group" "rg" {
  name     = "ApressAzureTerraformCH05"
  location = "southeastasia"
}

resource "azurerm_kubernetes_cluster" "akscluster" {
  name                = "aks"
  location            = azurerm_resource_group.rg.location
  resource_group_name = azurerm_resource_group.rg.name
  dns_prefix          = "aks"

  default_node_pool {
    name       = "default"
    node_count = var.node_count
    vm_size    = "Standard_D2_v2"
  }

  identity {
    type = "SystemAssigned"
  }

  tags = {
    Environment = "DEV"
  }
}
```

```
resource "azurerm_container_registry" "acr" {
  name                = "apresstfacr"
  resource_group_name = azurerm_resource_group.rg.name
  location            = azurerm_resource_group.rg.location
  sku                 = "Premium"
 admin_enabled        = true

}

resource "azurerm_role_assignment" "role" {
  principal_id                      = azurerm_kubernetes_cluster.akscluster.
                                      kubelet_identity[0].object_id

  role_definition_name              = "AcrPull"
  scope                             = azurerm_container_registry.acr.id
  skip_service_principal_aad_check = true
}
```

Once the cluster and image are deployed, we can push an image to the new registry using the steps we learned in Chapter 3.

Using the ACR Container Image with AKS

To pull a Docker container image from an ACR registry, all we need to do is modify the deployment.yaml file we used to deploy the nginx docker image. We can do so win this way:

1. Change the name of the image from nginx:latest to ch03/ image01:v1, or to the name of an image you have on your ACR registry, as follows:

```
- name: web-server
  image: ch03/image01:v1
  resources:
    requests:
      cpu: 100m
      memory: 128Mi
    limits:
      cpu: 250m
```

```
        memory: 256Mi
    ports:
    - containerPort: 80
      name: redis
```

2. Save the file, then deploy the application using the following kubectl command line:

```
kubectl apply -f deployment.yaml
```

3. To test the application, run the get service command with the name of the service:

```
kubectl get service web-server —watch
```

AKS Volumes

In this section, I will show you how to mount a persistent storage volume to AKS and use it with containerized applications. The process is like the one we used in Chapter 4, where we mounted a storage volume to our ACI deployment.

In AKS, we don't create the underlying storage account or volumes using Terraform; the entire process is done using the kubectl command line and the YAML configuration files.

In the following example, I will show you how to mount a persistent volume that can be dynamically provisioned to one or more pods. To create persistent storage volume using the following:

- Create_Storage_Class.yaml

- Create_Volume_Claim.yaml

- Create_Pod_With_Volume.yaml

Once the storage is configured and deployed, I will deploy the nginx web server and mount a persistent volume to it. All the data that is saved in the mounted storage will remain intact after I delete the pods.

Creating a Storage Class

The first step in configuring storage for an AKS cluster is to create an Azure file share as our underlying source of storage, as follows:

1. Deploy the following YAML file to hold the configuration of the storage class:

```
kind: StorageClass
apiVersion: storage.k8s.io/v1
metadata:
  name: my-azurefile
provisioner: file.csi.azure.com
allowVolumeExpansion: true
mountOptions:
  - dir_mode=0777
  - file_mode=0777
  - uid=0
  - gid=0
  - mfsymlinks
  - cache=strict
  - actimeo=30
parameters:
  skuName: Premium_LRS
```

2. Create a file named `Create_Storage_Class.yaml` and deploy it using the following cmdlet:

```
kubectl apply -f Create_Storage_Class.yaml
```

Once the storage class is ready, we'll create a volume claim.

Note   The storage class is using Standard_LRS storage, or locally redundant storage. If you'd like to use georedundant storage, use Standard_GRS.

Creating a Volume Claim

Next, we'll create a volume claim, also known as a persistent volume claim (PVC). This claim uses the storage class we created to dynamically provision storage volumes to pods.

1. To create the PVC, make a file called `Create_Volume_Claim.yaml` by using the following configuration:

```
apiVersion: v1
kind: PersistentVolumeClaim
metadata:
  name: my-azurefile
spec:
  accessModes:
    - ReadWriteMany
  storageClassName: my-azurefile
  resources:
    requests:
      storage: 100Gi
```

2. To create the claim, run the following command:

```
kubectl apply -f Create_Volume_Claim.yaml
```

3. You can check if the PVC was deployed by running the following kubectl command:

```
kubectl get pvc
```

Configuring a Pod to Use a Persistent Volume

Now that the persistent storage is configured, we can deploy a pod and mount a storage volume to it. That can be done like this:

1. Use the following YAML file:

```
kind: Pod
apiVersion: v1
metadata:
  name: mypod
```

```
      spec:
        containers:
          - name: mypod
            image: nginx:latest
            resources:
              requests:
                cpu: 100m
                memory: 128Mi
              limits:
                cpu: 250m
                memory: 256Mi
            volumeMounts:
              - mountPath: /mnt/azure
                name: volume
        volumes:
          - name: volume
            persistentVolumeClaim:
              claimName: my-azurefile
```

2. To deploy the pod, run the following command:

    ```
    kubectl apply -f Create_Pod_With_Volume.yaml
    ```

3. To test the deployment and see if the storage was mounted
    successfully, connect to the running pod using the `kubectl exec`
    command and start the bash shell utility using the `kubectl exec -it`
    `nginx -- /bin/bash` command.

Upgrading an AKS Cluster

As I mentioned at the beginning of this chapter, AKS is an Azure-managed service,
which means that Azure manages its underlying infrastructure. When it comes to
AKS management, Azure allows us to upgrade our AKS cluster to the latest version on
Kubernetes or wait for Microsoft to do the upgrade.

Some organizations choose to upgrade before the Microsoft update so that they can
use the new features faster and not have to wait for Microsoft.

To update our AKS cluster to the latest version of Kubernetes, any of the following tools can be used:

- Azure PowerShell

- Azure CLI

- Azure portal

In our case, we'll use the Azure CLI.

The process to update an AKS cluster is:

1. Check for available updates by using the following command:

```
az aks get-upgrades  --resource-group ApressAzureTerraformCH05
--name AKS -o table
```

2. The output of the command should show the following items: (a) the current version; and (b) available versions.

```
Name      ResourceGroup                  MasterVersion    Upgrades
-------   ------------------------       ---------------  --------------
default   ApressAzureTerraformCH05       1.26.6           1.27.1, 1.27.3
```

The command output shows that two updates are available (1.27.1 and 1.27.3) and ready for installation.

3. To update the cluster to version 1.27.1 of Kubernetes, run the following Azure CLI command:

```
az aks upgrade  --resource-group ApressAzureTerraformCH05 --name
AKS --kubernetes-version 1.27.3
```

4. After running the upgrade command, the following confirmation message will appear.

```
Kubernetes may be unavailable during cluster upgrades.
Are you sure you want to perform this operation? (y/N): y
Since control-plane-only argument is not specified, this will
upgrade the control plane AND all nodepools to version 1.27.3.
Continue? (y/N): y
```

5. After a few minutes, the cluster will run the latest version of Kubernetes.

Autoupgrading the AKS Cluster

If you want to automate the upgrade process so that you don't have to worry about doing it yourself, you can configure your AKS cluster to automatically upgrade.

To do so, we need to first decide which upgrade channel to configure our cluster to follow. Table 5-1 shows the channels that are available to select from.

Table 5-1. *Upgrade Channels That the AKS Cluster Can Follow*

Channel	Function
None	Disables autoupgrades (default).
Patch	Upgrades to the latest supported version of AKS as soon it becomes available.
Stable	Upgrades to the latest supported patch and uses version N-1.
Repid	Upgrades to the latest supported patch and minor version release.
Node-image	Upgrades the node-image to the latest version.

Once you decide which channel to use, open a terminal window and connect to AKS. Run the following command to configure auto-upgrade using the patch channel:

```
az aks update  --resource-group ApressAzureTerraformCH05 --name
AKS  --auto-upgrade-channel patch
```

You can also configure autoupgrade from the Azure portal by opening the AKS "Cluster configuration" page, as shown in Figure 5-2.

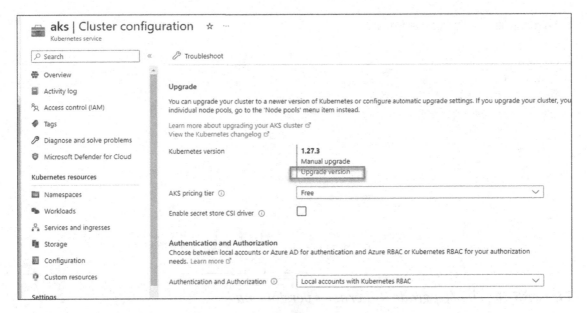

Figure 5-2. *Configuring autoupgrade with AKS "Cluster configuration"*

Use the following process for the AKS configuration:

1. Open the AKS cluster page from the Azure portal, Under the "Setting" option, click "Cluster configuration."

2. In the "Kubernetes version" section of the "Cluster configuration" page, click "Upgrade version."

3. On the "Upgrade Kubernetes version" page that appears, go to the "Automatic upgrade" drop-down list, as shown in Figure 5-3.

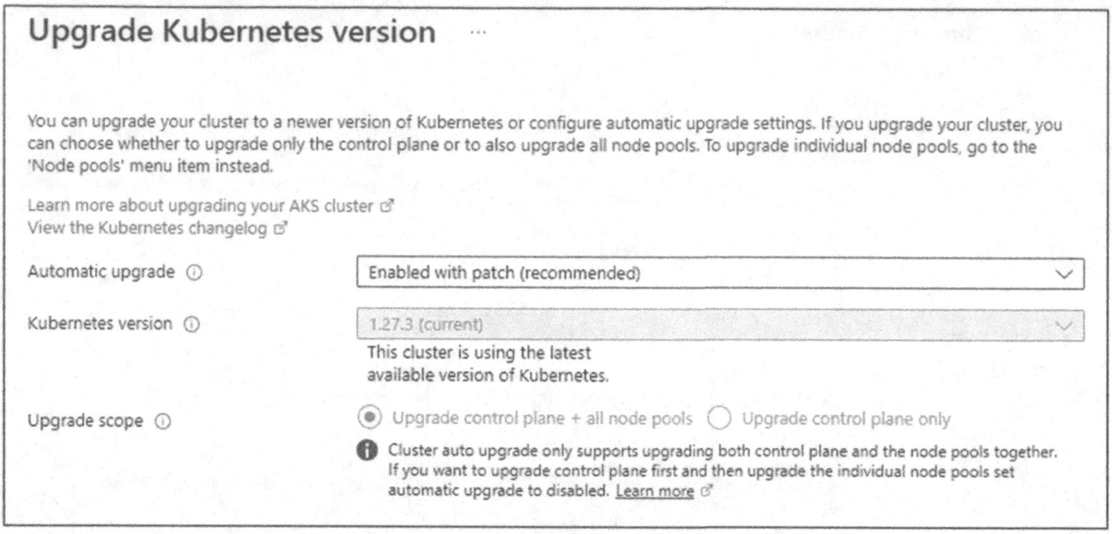

Upgrade Kubernetes version   ...

You can upgrade your cluster to a newer version of Kubernetes or configure automatic upgrade settings. If you upgrade your cluster, you can choose whether to upgrade only the control plane or to also upgrade all node pools. To upgrade individual node pools, go to the 'Node pools' menu item instead.

Learn more about upgrading your AKS cluster 🗗
View the Kubernetes changelog 🗗

Automatic upgrade ⓘ	Enabled with patch (recommended) ⌄
Kubernetes version ⓘ	1.27.3 (current) ⌄
	This cluster is using the latest available version of Kubernetes.
Upgrade scope ⓘ	⦿ Upgrade control plane + all node pools ◯ Upgrade control plane only

ⓘ Cluster auto upgrade only supports upgrading both control plane and the node pools together. If you want to upgrade control plane first and then upgrade the individual node pools set automatic upgrade to disabled. Learn more 🗗

Figure 5-3. *The "Upgrade Kubernetes version" page*

4. To disable autoupgrade, run the following command:

```
az aks update  --resource-group ApressAzureTerraformCH05 --name
AKS  --auto-upgrade-channel none
```

Terraform Remote State

Before we move on to the next chapter, I'd like to show you how to configure the Terraform remote state using Azure.

`terraform.tfstate` is a configuration file that holds the configuration of the Azure resources that were created with Terraform. The state file represents the current configuration in Azure.

It also serves as the source of truth for Azure resources that were created with Terraform. By default, the state file is stored locally in the directory where we run the Terraform commands to deploy resources.

The main challenges with a local state file is that it only exists locally, if something happens to the file we can't manage the environment using Terraform, and it doesn't allow collaboration between team members.

For these reasons, Terraform offers remote state management. With remote state management, the state file is stored in a shared location, and in our case, that location is an Azure storage account with file sharing enabled.

Once the remote state is configured, the following benefits will be available:

- *Collaboration*: Allows multiple team members to work on the same Terraform configuration simultaneously.

- *Versioning*: Allows users to track changes to infrastructure and roll back changes.

- *Security*: Provides encryption solutions to safeguard state files.

- *Automation*: Enables us to use continuous integration and continuous delivery (CI\CD) tools for infrastructure deployments.

- *Scalability*: Enables the scaling for the underlying storage of a state file.

Configuring the Remote State

To configure remote state management with Microsoft Azure, we'll take the following steps in Terraform:

- Creating a resource group

- Creating a storage account

- Creating a storage container

- Changing the state file location

- Adding the remote state to the configuration file and switching from the local state to the remote state

The process is as follows:

1. To get started, use the following Terraform configuration file:

```
resource "random_string" "resource_code" {
  length  = 5
  special = false
  upper   = false
```

```
    }

    resource "azurerm_resource_group" "tfstate" {
      name     = "chapter5remotestate"
      location = "southeastasia"
    }

    resource "azurerm_storage_account" "tfstate" {
      name                     = "tfstate${random_string.resource_
                                   code.result}"
      resource_group_name      = azurerm_resource_group.tfstate.name
      location                 = azurerm_resource_group.tfstate.
                                   location
      account_tier             = "Standard"
      account_replication_type = "LRS"

      tags = {
        environment = "dev"
      }
    }

    resource "azurerm_storage_container" "tfstate" {
      name                  = "tfstate"
      storage_account_name  = azurerm_storage_account.tfstate.name
      container_access_type = "blob"
    }
```

The remote storage configuration files are in the repository under
Chapter 5. Note that the configuration folder contains an output
file that will export the storage account name, which we'll need to
complete the configuration.

The output file looks like this:

```
data "azurerm_storage_account" "storage" {
  name                = azurerm_storage_account.tfstate.name
  resource_group_name = azurerm_resource_group.rg.name
}
```

```
output "storage_account_name" {
  value = azurerm_storage_account.tfstate.name
}
```

2. To start the deployment process, run:

    a. Terraform init

    b. Terraform plan

    c. Terraform apply

    The output should be:

    ```
    Apply complete! Resources: 4 added, 0 changed, 0 destroyed.
    Outputs:
    storage_account_name = "tfstateblf8x"
    ```

3. At this stage, we have a storage account that is ready to be used
    as a remote state. Note the storage account name, as we'll need it
    soon. We now need to copy the security key that will allow us to
    authenticate to the storage account and write the configuration.

    Use the following two commands to get the storage access key.
    Save the key as an environment variable.

    ```
    ACCOUNT_KEY=$(az storage account keys list --resource-group
    chapter5remotestate --account-name tfstateblf8x --query '[0].
    value' -o tsv)
    export ARM_ACCESS_KEY=$ACCOUNT_KEY
    ```

Adding Backend Configuration

The feature that allows us to store state files remotely is called backend configuration.
We'll need to add it to our Terraform configuration files.

A standard backend configuration file looks like this:

```
backend "azurerm" {
    resource_group_name  = "tfstate"
    storage_account_name = Storage_ACCOUNT_NAME
```

```
    container_name         = "storage_container_name"
    key                    = "keyname.terraform.tfstate"
}
```

In our case, this is how the configuration will look:

```
backend "azurerm" {
    resource_group_name  = "chapter5remotestate"
    storage_account_name = "tfstateblf8x"
    container_name       = "terraformstate"
    key                  = "0.storageaccount.terraform.tfstate"
}
```

You can find the configuration code in the provider.tf configuration file.
To set up backend configuration:

1. Create a new Terraform resource for a new storage account as
   outlined in the following code. (You can use the "repository
   configuration_block" folder to create a storage account).

   ```
   terraform {
     required_providers {
       azurerm = {
         source  = "hashicorp/azurerm"

       }
     }

     backend "azurerm" {
         resource_group_name  = "chapter5remotestate"
         storage_account_name = "tfstateblf8x"
         container_name       = "tfstate"
         key                  = "0.storageaccount.terraform.tfstate"
     }

   }

   provider "azurerm" {

     features {
       key_vault {
   ```

144

```
        purge_soft_delete_on_destroy = true
      }
    }

  }
```

2. Run the following command and review the output to confirm that Terraform is using a remote state file.

```
Terraform init
```

3. Check the output and notice and review the third line (start with "use this backend...").

```
Initializing the backend...

Successfully configured the backend "azurerm"! Terraform will automatically
use this backend unless the backend configuration changes.

Initializing provider plugins...
- Finding latest version of hashicorp/azurerm...
- Finding latest version of hashicorp/random...
- Installing hashicorp/azurerm v3.71.0...
- Installed hashicorp/azurerm v3.71.0 (signed by HashiCorp)
- Installing hashicorp/random v3.5.1...
- Installed hashicorp/random v3.5.1 (signed by HashiCorp)

Terraform has created a lock file .terraform.lock.hcl to record the
provider selections it made above. Include this file in your version
control repository so that Terraform can guarantee to make the same
selections by default when you run "terraform init" in the future.

Terraform has been successfully initialized!

You may now begin working with Terraform. Try running "terraform plan" to
see any changes that are required for your infrastructure. All Terraform
commands should now work.

If you ever set or change modules or backend configuration for Terraform,
rerun this command to reinitialize your working directory. If you forget,
other commands will detect it and remind you to do so if necessary.
Continue with the deployment and run
```

```
terraform plan
terraform apply
```

Once the deployment is complete, open the Azure portal and navigate to the storage account.

```
Click on Storage account
Click on Containers
Click on tfstate
```

4. Review the Azure state file, as shown in Figure 5-4.

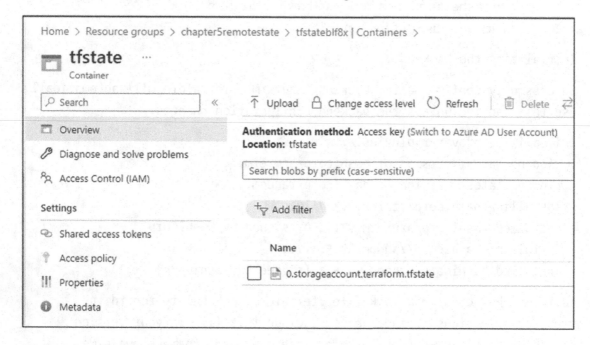

Figure 5-4. *Reviewing the Azure state file*

State Locking

To prevent two users from deploying resources to Azure at the same time, Azure storage blobs will automatically lock the state file before any write operation. To check whether a remote state file is locked, you can take the following steps:

1. Open the storage account from the Azure Portal.

2. Click "Containers."

3. Click "tfstate."

4. Click the state file for which you want to check the status.

5. Look for the "LEASE STATUS" field on the blob storage page and check the whether it is locked, as shown in Figure 5-5.

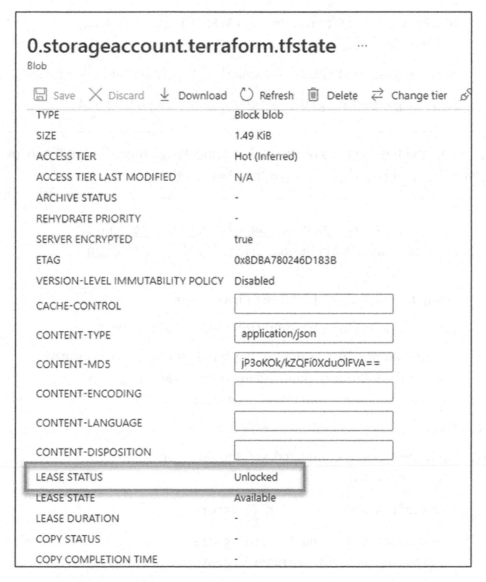

Figure 5-5. *"LEASE STATUS" field*

Exporting Azure Resources to Terraform

Before wrapping up this chapter, I'd like to discuss a scenario where Azure resources are created using the Azure portal or Azure CLI and you want to manage them with Terraform.

For instances like these, Azure created a tool called `aztfexport` that allows us to export Azure resources to Terraform.

To do so:

1. Install the `aztfexport` tool on Linux WSL using the following commands:

   a. `sudo snap install go --channel=1.19-fips/stable --classic`

   b. `sudo go install github.com/Azure/aztfexport@latest`

Note   To install the "`aztfexport`" tool on Windows or macOS, visit the following URL: `https://github.com/azure/aztfexport`.

---

2. To export a resource that was created using a non-Terraform tool, create a directory on your machine and open it using a terminal window.

3. Log in to Azure using the Azure CLI: `Az login`.

4. Create the following empty directory: `sudo mkdir export`.

5. Note the name of the resource group where the resource is located and run the following command to export a resource group configuration: `aztfexport resource-group RGNAME`.

6. Press the *w* key to confirm the export.

7. Once the export is completed, you should see the following output:

`Microsoft Azure Export for Terraform`

   `Terraform state and the config are generated at: /home/shimon/ github/ApressAzureTerraform/chapter05/aztfimport`

   `Press any key to quit`

8. Once the configuration is exported to the directory, run the following command:

```
terraform init  --upgrade

terraform plan
```

9. If the export was successful, you should see the following output from the Terraform plan command:

```
No changes. Your infrastructure matches the
configuration.

Terraform has compared your real infrastructure against your
configuration and found no differences, so no changes are needed.
```

If you get this output, you can now manage the resource using Terraform.

Summary

In this chapter, we learned how to do the following: (1) deploy an AKS cluster; (2) connect an AKS cluster to the Azure Container Registry; (3) mount a storage volume to AKS pods; (3) upgrade the AKS cluster using a manual process or autoupgrade; (4) use the Terraform remote state to store configuration files; and (5) export Azure resources to Terraform.

Azure DevOps and Container Service

Introduction

Now that we've learned about all the container services Azure has to offer, it's time to look at how we can use continuous integration and continuous delivery (CI/CD) tools like Azure DevOps to deploy and automate infrastructure using Azure Pipelines.

This chapter will dive into the integration between Azure DevOps and Terraform and explore how infrastructure provisioning can be automated using CI/CD tools.

As Azure cloud resource environments become more complex and integrated with one another, performing manual changes and configuration is no longer viable. Because of this reason, Azure DevOps provides a platform for defining and provisioning infrastructure as code to help with rapid deployment and repeatability.

Using examples and step-by-step guides, in this chapter we will explore how Azure DevOps and Terraform complement each other and make infrastructure management more consistent and rapid.

The goal of this chapter is to help you learn how to optimize resource provisioning and management using Azure DevOps tools.

Azure DevOps Services

Azure DevOps offers a comprehensive suite of DevOps tools that improve the collaboration between and delivery of software and infrastructure services.

151

© Shimon Ifrah 2023
S. Ifrah, *Getting Started with Containers in Azure*, https://doi.org/10.1007/978-1-4842-9972-2_6

The main services the Azure DevOps platform offers are:

- *Version control*: Azure Repos services offer version control capabilities using secure Git repositories with the following features:

  - branch management

  - code review

  - code merging

  - change history

  - code approval

- *Continuous integration and continuous delivery*: Azure Pipelines offers a powerful CI/CD solution using YAML files that allows us to:

  - build code and docker images

  - test code and use cases

  - deploy infrastructure to Azure or other cloud providers using Terraform

  - create workflows

- *Agile planning and tracking*: Azure Boards enables teams to manage projects using agile project management tools. With Boards, you can:

  - create and manage user stories

  - create and track work items

  - create and plan sprints

  - get real-time insights into the progress of projects

  - allocate resources

- *Automated testing*: Azure Test Plans enables testing and monitoring of services using automation.

In summary, Azure DevOps allows the collaboration between building and deployment of software, services, and infrastructure using automation and state-of-the-art tools. This chapter will focus on deploying infrastructure using automation to Azure.

Setting Up Azure DevOps

Before getting started, you'll need to sign up for an Azure DevOps account and set up an Azure DevOps organization. To do so, go to the Azure DevOps home page at `https://azure.microsoft.com/en-us/products/devops/` and click "Start free," as shown in Figure 6-1.

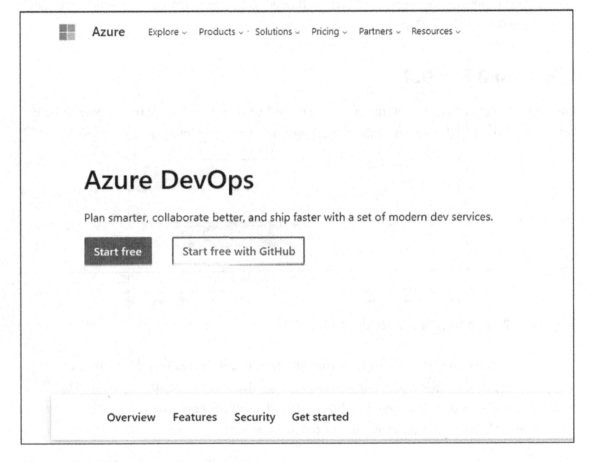

Figure 6-1. *The Azure DevOps sign-up page*

After signing up for Azure DevOps, you'll need to create an organization to host your projects.

Creating an Azure DevOps Organization

To complete the sign-up process, create an organization and make note of your organization's name. The login URL to Azure DevOps is made up of the host web site plus your organization's name as follows: `https://dev.azure.com/`[name of your organization].

To host pipelines and repositories, you'll need to create a project that acts as a logical unit for all the services a DevOps project needs.

Creating a Project

Once you log into Azure DevOps, you can create a project by clicking the "+ New Project" button in the top right corner of the main page, as shown in Figure 6-2.

Figure 6-2. *Creating a new project*

In the "Create new project" screen that appears, enter the required information, as shown in Figure 6-3. Also note that you can change the version control system to the team foundation server and select a different work item process that uses Agile, Basic, Scrum, or CMMI (computer maturity model integration).

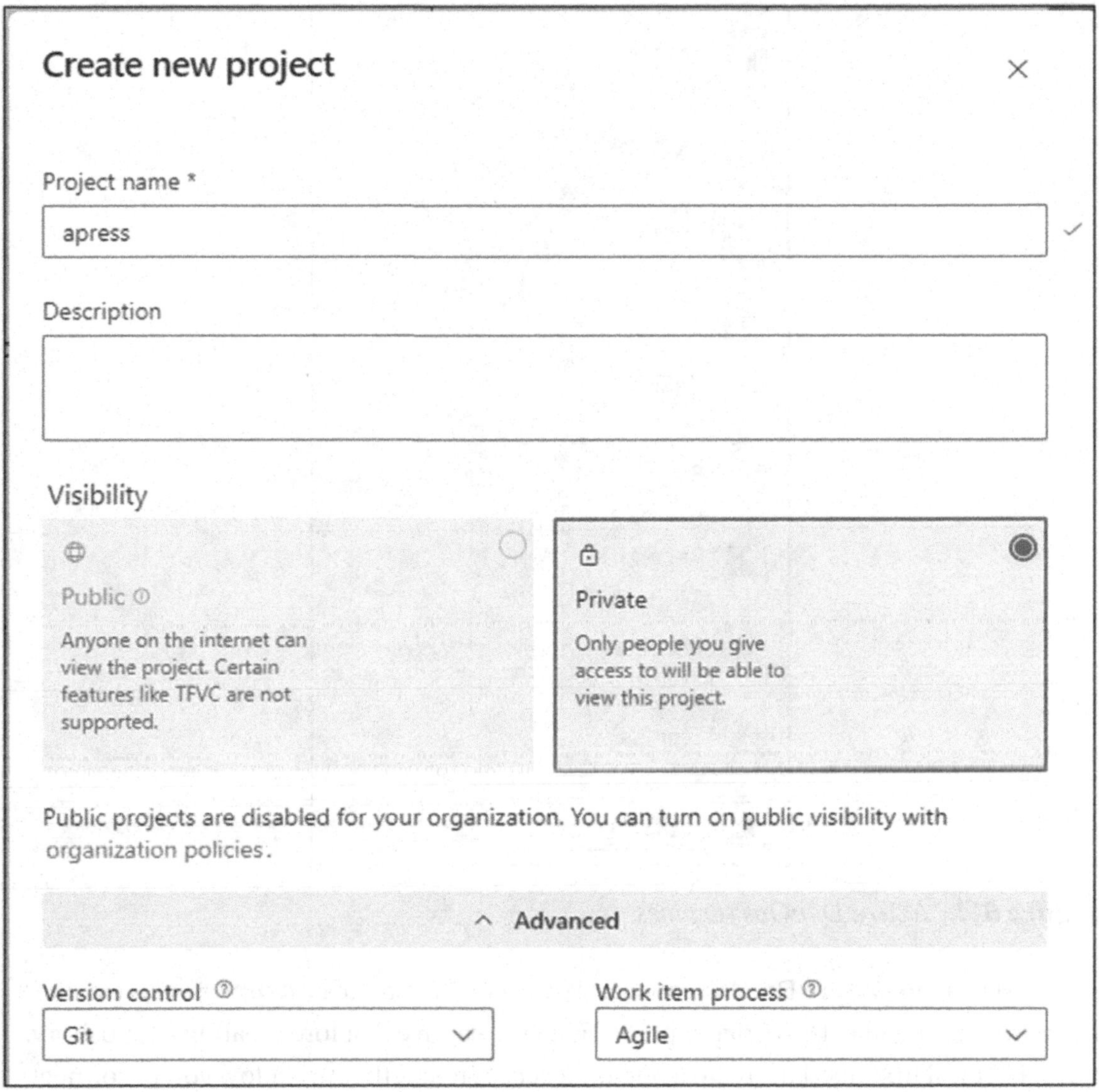

Create new project ✕

Project name *

apress ✓

Description

Visibility

⊕

Public ⓘ ○

Anyone on the internet can
view the project. Certain
features like TFVC are not
supported.

🔒

Private ◉

Only people you give
access to will be able to
view this project.

Public projects are disabled for your organization. You can turn on public visibility with
organization policies.

∧ Advanced

Version control ⑦

Git ⌄

Work item process ⑦

Agile ⌄

Figure 6-3. *Entering the required information for your new Azure DevOps project*

Once the project has been created, you can start using it. On the main project page,
you'll see all the available services that can be used to deploy and manage services, as
shown in Figure 6-4.

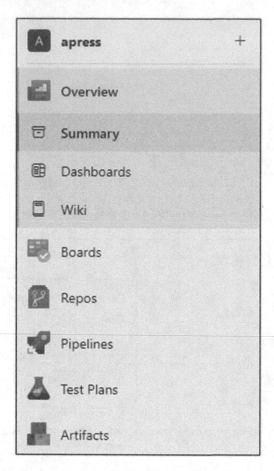

Figure 6-4. *Azure DevOps services*

To start using Azure DevOps services, you'll need to create or define a source code repository that will act as a trigger point for all the services. Before creating a repository, though, you'll first need to create a personal access token that will allow you to connect to Azure DevOps programmatically.

Creating a Personal Access Token

Before creating a repository, we'll need to create a personal access token (PAT) that will allow us to authenticate easily to the service. To create a PAT:

1. Click the user settings icon located in the top-right corner of the screen, as shown in Figure 6-5.

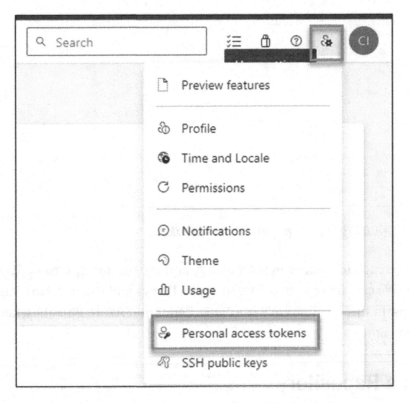

Figure 6-5. Selecting "Personal access tokens" on the drop-down menu

2. Select "Personal access tokens" from the drop-down menu that appears, as shown in Figure 6-5.

3. Then, click "New token" on the "Personal Access Tokens" page to create a new token. Figure 6-6 shows the "Create a new personal access token" screen. In this example, we'll create a token that gives us full access to all the Azure DevOps services.

4. On this screen, add a name for your token, select your organization and the token expiration date from the drop-down lists, and set "Scopes" to full access, as shown in Figure 6-6.

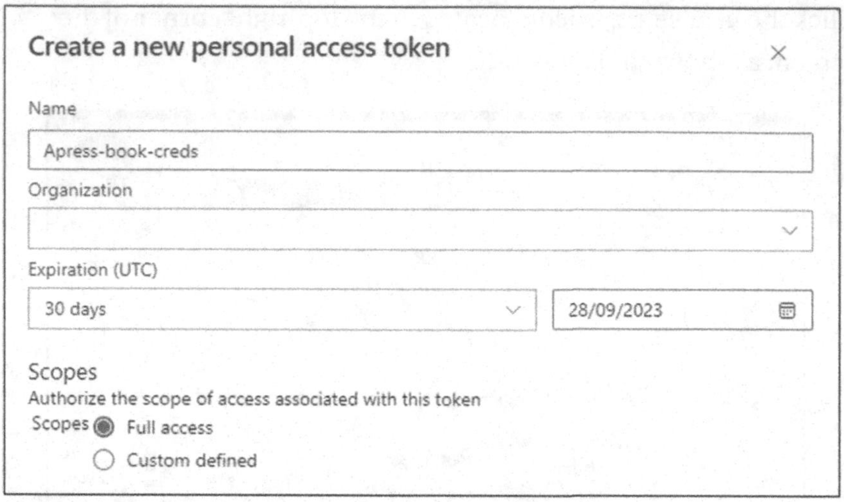

Figure 6-6. *Creating a new personal access token*

Now we're ready to create a new repository and use our newly created PAT to authenticate. We can also create secure shell (SSH) keys and use them to authenticate to Azure DevOps. In this chapter, we'll use Azure Repos and Azure Pipelines. Let's start by creating a repository.

Creating a Repository

To create a repository in which to store our code, we will use Azure Repos; however, if you prefer to use another source-control service like GitHub, it's probably also possible to connect to its repository.

To create the repository:

1. Click "Repos" on the project page you just created.

2. Because we haven't initialized a repository, you'll be taken the general repository page, allowing you to clone, push, or import a repository, as shown in Figure 6-7. Go ahead and click the "copy" icon next to HTTPS repository URL and then hit the "Initialize" button at the bottom of the page.

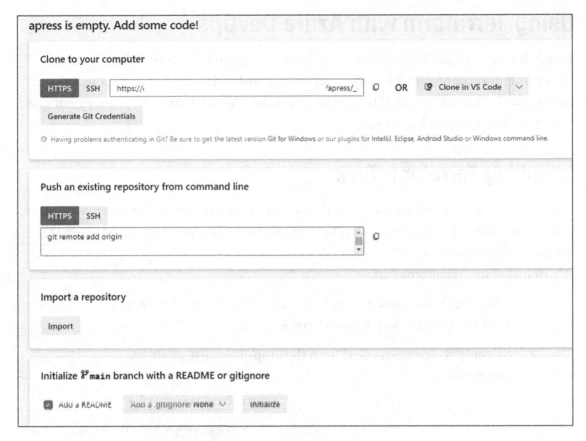

Figure 6-7. *Initializing the Azure repository*

3. Now open Visual Studio Code.

4. Create a new directory.

5. Run the following command to clone the new repository:

   ```
   git clone copied_url
   ```

6. Once you run the command, you'll be asked to provide the PAT password in order to authenticate and pull the repository.

Using Terraform with Azure DevOps

To use Terraform with Azure DevOps, we need to install the Terraform Task for Azure DevOps. The Terraform Task has the integration capabilities needed to work with Azure DevOps with minimum code. The integration makes the infrastructure deployment task straightforward, as you'll soon see.

Installing Terraform Task

To install the Terraform Task for Azure DevOps, we'll use the Azure DevOps marketplace, which has tasks that allow Azure DevOps to work with external services and integrate with tools like Terraform.

To install the Terraform Task:

1. Click the "Marketplace" icon in the top-right corner of the Azure DevOps organization or project page.

2. Select "Browse extensions" from the drop-down list, as shown in Figure 6-8.

Figure 6-8. *Azure DevOps marketplace*

3. On the "Marketplace" home page, type "terraform" into the search bar. In the results that come up, click the "Terraform" option, offered by Microsoft DevLabs, as shown in Figure 6-9.

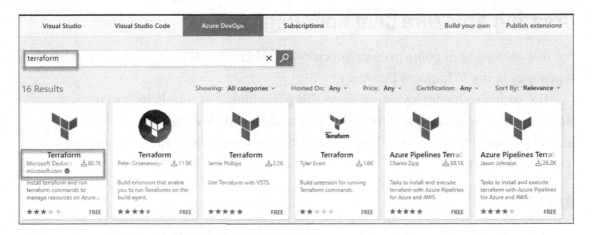

Figure 6-9. *Choosing the Terraform option*

On the Terraform page that comes up, click "Get for free" to install the extension in the Azure DevOps organization and make it available with Azure Pipelines.

Azure Pipelines

In this section, we're going to explore how to use Azure Pipelines and use a CI/CD pipeline to deploy an Azure Container Registry to Azure directly from the pipeline.

For this exercise to work, we'll utilize some of the previous concepts we learned in this book and incorporate them into a single learning exercise, as you'll see shortly.

In the exercise, we'll do the following:

- use the Terraform configuration file to create an ACR on Azure

- use a remote stage file (as done in the Chapter 5)

- use a YAML-based CI/CD pipeline

- use an Azure pipeline

We'll need to use a Terraform remote state file for this exercise to work successfully. When using Azure Pipelines, the pipeline runs on a temporary virtual machine that gets destroyed once the pipeline has finished running. If the state is saved on that machine, we could manage the resources postdeployment.

Creating an Azure Container Registry

For this exercise, I'm going to use a directory called Create_ACR, which is in the book's repository in the "Chapter 6 Directory."

The code for the deployment follows this paragraph. For simplicity, I'm using a single file for this deployment; however, you could break down the file easily. Take a look at the backend section and replace the remote state details with your remote state (created in Chapter 5).

ACR.TF

The following file will configure an Azure Container registry (ACR).

```
terraform {

required_providers {
azurerm = {
source  = "hashicorp/azurerm"
version = ">= 2.26"
}
}

backend "azurerm" {
resource_group_name   = "tfstate"
storage_account_name  = "tfstates14w8"
container_name        = "tfstate"
key                   = "Create_acr.terraform.tfstate"
}

}

provider "azurerm" {
features {}
}

resource "azurerm_resource_group" "rg" {
name     = "apresstfchapter06"
location = "australiasoutheast"
}
```

```
resource "azurerm_container_registry" "acr" {
name                = "appressacr"
resource_group_name = azurerm_resource_group.rg.name
location            = azurerm_resource_group.rg.location
sku                 = "Basic"
admin_enabled       = true
}
```

AZURE-PIPELINES.YML

What follows is the code the YAML-based pipeline file that will handle the deployment to Microsoft Azure and use the Terraform extension for Azure DevOps:

```
trigger:
- none

pool:
  vmImage: ubuntu-latest

steps:
- task: TerraformInstaller@0
  inputs:
    terraformVersion: 'latest'
- task: TerraformTaskV3@3
  inputs:
    provider: 'azurerm'
    command: 'init'
    workingDirectory: '$(System.DefaultWorkingDirectory)/Create_ACR'
    backendServiceArm: 'AZURE SUBSCRIPTION DETAILS'
    backendAzureRmResourceGroupName: 'tfstate'
    backendAzureRmStorageAccountName: 'tfstates14w8'
    backendAzureRmContainerName: 'tfstate'
    backendAzureRmKey: 'Create_acr.terraform.tfstate'

- task: TerraformTaskV3@3
  inputs:
    provider: 'azurerm'
    command: 'plan'
```

```
  workingDirectory: '$(System.DefaultWorkingDirectory)/chapter06/
  Create_ACR'
  environmentServiceNameAzureRM: 'AZURE SUBSCRIPTION DETAILS''
- task: TerraformTaskV3@3
  inputs:
    provider: 'azurerm'
    command: 'apply'
    workingDirectory: '$(System.DefaultWorkingDirectory)/Create_ACR'
    environmentServiceNameAzureRM: 'AZURE SUBSCRIPTION DETAILS''
```

If you review the file, you'll see that it is using three Terraform tasks to do the following:

- initiate Terraform and connect to the remote state file.

- run `terraform plan`. You don't have to use this step, but having it there for reference and review is nice.

- run `terraform apply`. This will deploy the previous code to an Azure subscription.

Note   An important thing to note is that you'll need to configure the connection point to your Azure subscription, which we'll do shortly. For this exercise to work, you'll need to have contributor access to an Azure subscription at a minimum.

Once you save the two files, go ahead and push the repository to the Azure Repo by running the following command from the repository's main folder

```
git add .
git commit -m "Add Pipeline and ACR deployment"
git push
```

Note   To make things easier, you can copy the files in Chapter 6 to your Azure DevOps repository.

Creating an Azure Pipeline

Once the code has been pushed to Azure Repos, we'll be ready to create an Azure pipeline that will deploy an ACR to Azure.

To do so:

1. From the Azure DevOps portal, click on "Pipelines" on the Azure DevOps project page.

2. Click "Create Pipeline."

3. On the "Connect Repository" page, click "Azure Repos Git," as shown in Figure 6-10.

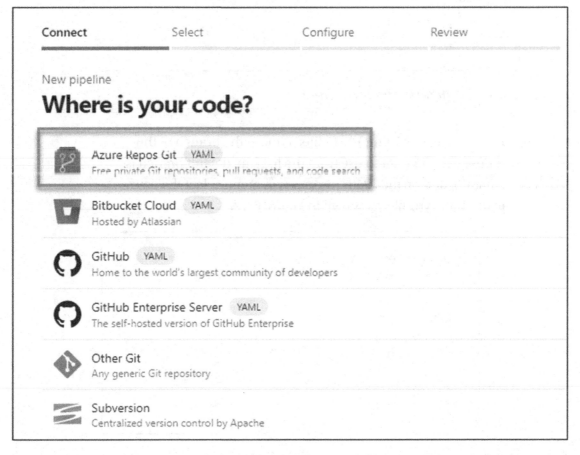

Figure 6-10. *Selecting "Azure Repos Git"*

4. In the "Configure" section of the "New pipeline" page, click the "Existing Azure Pipelines YAML file," as shown in Figure 6-11.

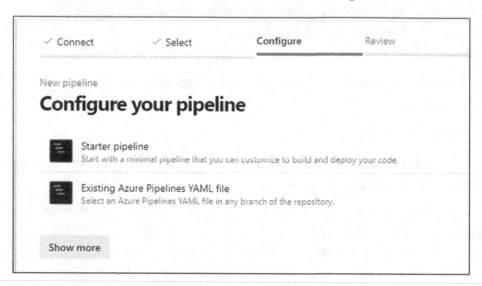

Figure 6-11. *Configuring your pipeline*

5. For "Select an Existing YAML file," choose the branch of the repository you want to use from the list (the default branch is "main"), and on the "Path" drop-down menu select the azure-pipelines.yml file, as shown in Figure 6-12.

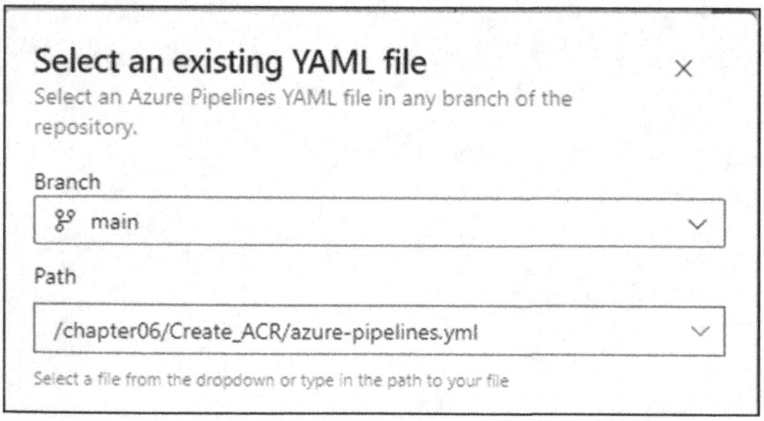

Figure 6-12. *Selecting the "Azure Pipelines YAML" file*

6. Once the pipeline is loading, we'll need to configure the Azure DevOps connection point to Azure to allow Azure DevOps to change resources. On the "Review your pipeline YAML" page, above the Terraform tasks, click "Settings," as shown in Figure 6-13.

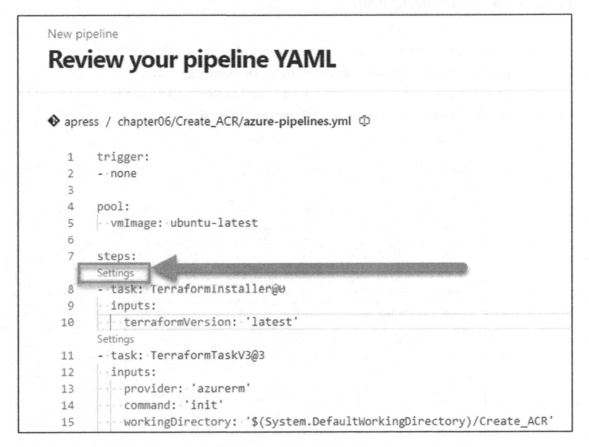

Figure 6-13. *The Terraform task settings*

7. Next, on the task's settings page, locate the Azure subscription section.

8. On the drop-down menu, click the Azure subscription you'd like to use to deploy the resource and click "Authorize." Figure 6-14 shows the menu of subscriptions.

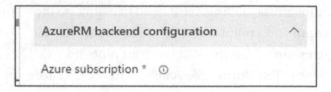

Figure 6-14. *Choosing the Azure subscription*

9. Now, take a few moments to review the configuration of the
    pipeline and the Terraform tasks. Once your service connections
    to Azure are ready, click the "Save and run" button and fill in the
    sections to commit the code, as shown in Figure 6-15.

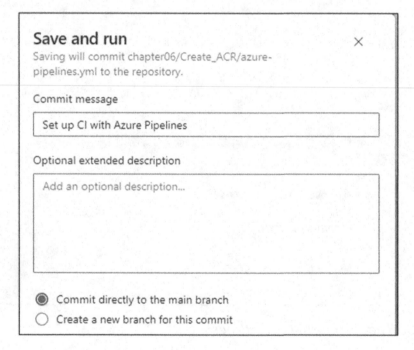

Figure 6-15. *The "Save and run" pipeline*

Note   If you receive a message that the pipeline must be authorized, click the
"Resources Authorized" button to continue.

Reviewing the Pipeline

Once the pipeline starts running, you can review the tasks that are involved by clicking the job name in the "Jobs" section. The "Jobs in run" page will list all the stages and tasks the pipeline is going through and the status of each one, as shown in Figure 6-16.

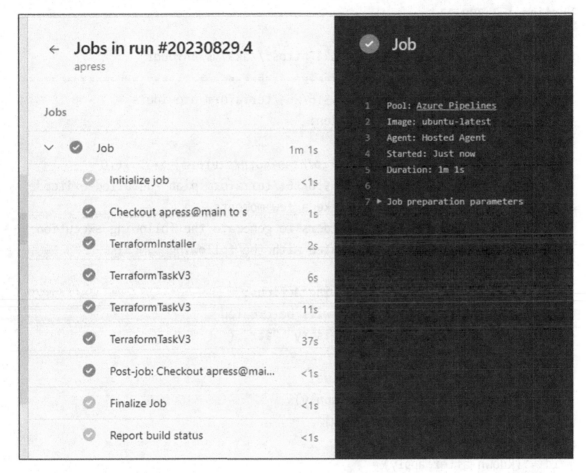

Figure 6-16. *List of the stages and tasks of the pipeline on the "Jobs in run" page*

Clicking on one of the tasks will reveal the deployment detail and what Azure DevOps is doing in order to deploy the code from the runner machine. The following output shows the Terraform plan task in detail:

Starting: TerraformTaskV3

```
================================================================================
Task : Terraform
Description : Execute terraform commands to manage resources on AzureRM,
Amazon Web Services(AWS) and Google Cloud Platform(GCP)
Version : 3.209.23
Author : Microsoft Corporation
Help : [Learn more about this task](https://aka.ms/AAfOuqr)
================================================================================
/opt/hostedtoolcache/terraform/1.5.6/x64/terraform providers
Providers required by configuration:
.
└── provider[registry.terraform.io/hashicorp/azurerm] >= 2.26.0
/opt/hostedtoolcache/terraform/1.5.6/x64/terraform plan -detailed-exitcode
Acquiring state lock. This may take a few moments...
Terraform used the selected providers to generate the following execution
plan. Resource actions are indicated with the following symbols:
+ create
Terraform will perform the following actions:
# azurerm_container_registry.acr will be created
+ resource "azurerm_container_registry" "acr" {
+ admin_enabled = true
+ admin_password = (sensitive value)
+ admin_username = (known after apply)
+ encryption = (known after apply)
+ export_policy_enabled = true
+ id = (known after apply)
+ location = "australiasoutheast"
+ login_server = (known after apply)
+ name = "appressacr"
+ network_rule_bypass_option = "AzureServices"
+ network_rule_set = (known after apply)
+ public_network_access_enabled = true
+ resource_group_name = "apresstfchapter06"
+ retention_policy = (known after apply)
+ sku = "Basic"
```

To make sure the resource was created, open the Azure portal and locate the resource group called "apresstfchapter06" and confirm that you have an ACR registry called "apressacr," as shown in Figure 6-17.

Figure 6-17. *The ACR registry*

At this stage, we have an ACR registry up and running in Azure that we've deployed with an Azure DevOps pipeline. Let's go another step further and use Azure Pipelines to build a Docker image using the Dockerfile we used in Chapter 3. In this exercise, we'll complete the following tasks:

- building a Docker image using a Dockerfile with Azure Pipeline

- pushing the image to an ACR

Building and Pushing a Docker Image to ACR with Azure Pipelines

For this exercise, I'm going to use the same Dockerfile as the one we used in Chapter 3. The Dockerfile shown here is simple:

```
FROM mcr.microsoft.com/hello-world
```

Follow these steps:

1. Copy the Dockerfile to the repository where your Terraform configuration file is located, and push the changes to the repository.

2. Create a new pipeline by clicking "New Pipeline" on the "Pipelines" page, as shown in Figure 6-18.

171

Figure 6-18. *Creating a new pipeline*

3. Now, select the repository and click "Next." On the "Configure your pipeline" page, you'll see that Azure DevOps is smart enough to have detected the Dockerfile and suggested a few pipelines you can choose from, as shown in Figure 6-19.

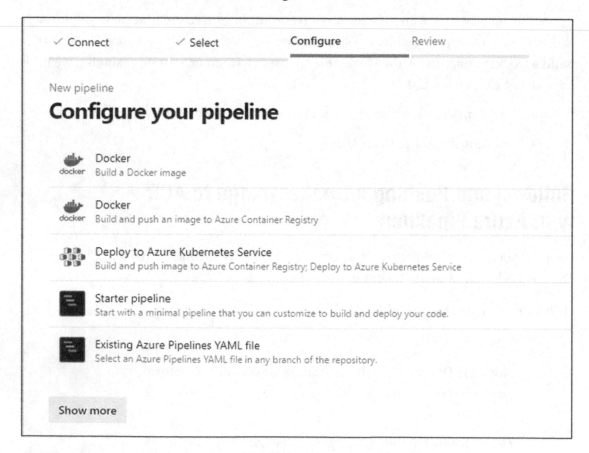

Figure 6-19. *Configuring your pipeline*

4. For this exercise, let's go ahead and select the second pipeline, "Docker - Build and push an image to Azure Container Registry."

5. After indicating the pipeline, you'll need to select the subscription in which the ACR registry is located. Figure 6-20 shows the "Select an Azure subscription" button.

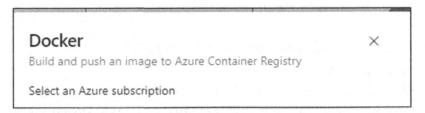

Figure 6-20. *Selecting an Azure subscription*

6. In the "Docker" menu, shown in Figure 6-21, select the Azure Container Registry details we deployed earlier: the image name and the Dockerfile.

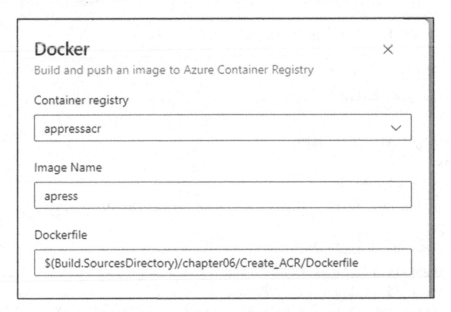

Figure 6-21. *Selecting the ACR details on the "Docker" screen*

The next screen will display the generated YAML pipeline, which looks like this:

```
trigger:
- main

resources:
- repo: self

variables:
  dockerRegistryServiceConnection: AZURE SUBSCRIPTION
  imageRepository: 'apress'
  containerRegistry: 'appressacr.azurecr.io'
  dockerfilePath: '$(Build.SourcesDirectory)/chapter06/Create_ACR/
Dockerfile'
  tag: '$(Build.BuildId)'

  vmImageName: 'ubuntu-latest'

stages:
- stage: Build
  displayName: Build and push stage
  jobs:
  - job: Build
    displayName: Build
    pool:
      vmImage: $(vmImageName)
    steps:
    - task: Docker@2
      displayName: Build and push an image to container registry
      inputs:
        command: buildAndPush
        repository: $(imageRepository)
        dockerfile: $(dockerfilePath)
        containerRegistry: $(dockerRegistryServiceConnection)
        tags: |
          $(tag)
```

7. Review the pipeline and try to understand the Docker task with which you'll build and push the image to ACR. Before you save and run the file, take a moment to rename the pipeline as shown in Figure 6-22. Click the "Rename" button and name the pipeline "buildAndPushACR.yml."

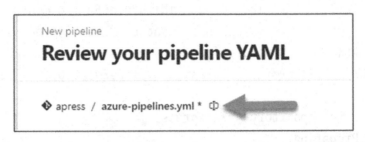

Figure 6-22. *Build and push an image to Azure Container Registry*

The output of the "Build and push to ACR" should look like this:

```
#5 exporting layers done
#5 writing image sha256:81a0f1bfdcc3147c40fa02caccd76c72fd78a6fed1c60d1fa64
6ae4205129db7 done
#5 naming to ***/apress:284 done
#5 DONE 0.0s
##[warning]No data was written into the file /home/vsts/work/_temp/task_
outputs/build_1693287997921.txt
/usr/bin/docker images
/usr/bin/docker push ***/apress:284
```

REPOSITORY	TAG	IMAGE ID	CREATED	SIZE
node	16	ebdc80ddefea	12 days ago	909MB
node	18	95d8a703ee8c	12 days ago	1.09GB
buildpack-deps	buster	0053f1bb059a	12 days ago	802MB
buildpack-deps	bullseye	eac77ea4e8a0	12 days ago	833MB
debian	10	de08540e8ff0	13 days ago	114MB
debian	11	07585eb55737	13 days ago	124MB
node	16-alpine	2573171e0124	2 weeks ago	118MB
node	18-alpine	50c7e33a9de1	2 weeks ago	176MB
alpine	3.16	187eae39ad94	3 weeks ago	5.54MB
alpine	3.17	1e0b8b5322fc	3 weeks ago	7.05MB

```
alpine                        3.18          7e01a0d0a1dc     3 weeks ago     7.33MB
ubuntu                        22.04         01f29b872827     3 weeks ago     77.8MB
moby/buildkit                 latest        896276ced360     3 weeks ago     172MB
ubuntu                        20.04         6df894023726     3 weeks ago     72.8MB
ubuntu                        18.04         f9a80a55f492     3 months ago    63.2MB
node                          14            1d12470fa662     4 months ago    912MB
node                          14-alpine     0dac3dc27b1a     5 months ago    119MB
***/apress       284          81a0f1bfdcc3     4 years ago      1.84kB
mcr.microsoft.com/hello-world    latest       fce289e99eb9     4 years
ago      1.84kB
The push refers to repository [***/apress]
af0b15c8625b: Preparing
af0b15c8625b: Pushed
284: digest: sha256:2ba0a8fbb31723c4afcd284bb26e1e48d01cb3e04cdef07b0311f3c
ae9c3da8f size: 524
```

```
/usr/bin/docker history --format createdAt:{{.CreatedAt}}; layerSize:{{.
Size}}; createdBy:{{.CreatedBy}}; layerId:{{.ID}} --no-trunc ***/apress:284
createdAt:2019-01-01T01:29:27Z; layerSize:0B; createdBy:/bin/sh -c
#(nop)  CMD ["/hello"]; layerId:sha256:81a0f1bfdcc3147c40fa02caccd76c72fd7
8a6fed1c60d1fa646ae4205129db7
createdAt:2019-01-01T01:29:27Z; layerSize:1.84kB; createdBy:/bin/sh -c
#(nop) COPY file:f77490f70ce51da25bd21bfc30cb5e1a24b2b65eb37d4af0c327ddc2
4f0986a6 in / ; layerId:<missing>
/usr/bin/docker inspect
81a0f1bfdcc3147c40fa02caccd76c72fd78a6fed1c60d1fa646ae4205129db7 -f
{{.RootFS.Layers}}
[sha256:af0b15c8625bb1938f1d7b17081031f649fd14e6b233688eea3c5483994a66a3]
Finishing: Build and push an image to container registry
```

8.   At this stage, the only thing left to do is to check whether the image
     is available in ACR. Do that by opening the Azure portal and
     checking the ACR repository, as shown in Figure 6-23.

Figure 6-23. *Checking whether the image is available in ACR*

Before we finish the chapter, I'd like to discuss the option of destroying resources with Azure DevOps. We can also use Azure Pipelines to destroy a Terraform deployment, and as a reference, I have provided the following code block you can use in another YAML pipeline to destroy a deployment.

Using Terraform Destroy with Azure Pipelines

To run the code, you can take the `apply` pipeline we used to deploy an ACR registry and replace the last task (`apply`) with the following code:

```
- task: TerraformTaskV3@3
  inputs:
    provider: 'azurerm'
    command: 'destroy'
    workingDirectory: '$(System.DefaultWorkingDirectory)/Create_ACR'
    environmentServiceNameAzureRM: 'AZURE SUBSCRIPTION'
```

The AzAPI Provider

In this last section of the chapter, I'd like to introduce you to the AzAPI provider and its capabilities in terms of managing Azure resources with Terraform. As you know, the Azure Terraform provider relies on supported features that Microsoft releases via the Azure representational state transfer (REST) API.

The issue with this is that Terraform isn't capable of new features that haven't yet been released or are in private or public preview. In some cases, because of Terraform's limitations it can't manage any aspect of a resource.

The AzAPI provider allows us to communicate directly with the Azure REST API and access all the API features, including preview features.

In the following exercise, we're going to deploy an ACR using the AzAPI provider.

Deploying an ACR Using the AzAPI Provider

To take part in this exercise, you'll need to open and use the Terraform configuration file under Chapter 6 and in the AzAPI folder. Let's first review the code before deploying it.

The first code block I'd like you to review is in the provider section, where we need to include the AzAPI provider:

```
terraform {

  required_providers {
    azurerm = {
      source  = "hashicorp/azurerm"
    }

    azapi = {
        source = "Azure/azapi"
    }

  }
}

provider "azurerm" {
  features {}
}

provider "azapi" {
}
```

The second code block that needs attention is the one where we configure the provider to connect to the Azure REST API. The API service we're connecting to is shown in Table 6-1.

Table 6-1. *Azure Container Registry REST API version details*

Service name	Container Registry
API version	2023-01-01-preview
Reference URL	https://learn.microsoft.com/en-us/rest/api/ containerregistry/registries/create?tabs=HTTP

The Terraform code that uses the service with AzAPI provider follows:

```
resource "azapi_resource" "acr" {
  type      = "Microsoft.ContainerRegistry/registries@2023-01-01-preview"
  name      = "apressacr"
  parent_id = azurerm_resource_group.rg.id
  location = azurerm_resource_group.rg.location

  body = jsonencode({
    sku = {
      name = "Standard"
    }
    properties = {
      adminUserEnabled = true
    }
  })

  tags = {
    "Key" = "DEV"
  }

  response_export_values = ["properties.loginServer", "properties.policies.
  quarantinePolicy.status"]
}
```

If you look at the code and API in the reference URL provided in Table 6-1, you'll see how the configuration calculates the API version and endpoint.

Full Code

You can review the full code and deploy it to Azure using Terraform. The deployment process is the same as any we've used before.

```
terraform {

  required_providers {
    azurerm = {
      source  = "hashicorp/azurerm"
    }

    azapi = {
        source = "Azure/azapi"
    }

  }
}

provider "azurerm" {
  features {}
}

provider "azapi" {
}

resource "azurerm_resource_group" "rg" {
  name     = "apresstfchapter06"
  location = "australiasoutheast"
}

resource "azapi_resource" "acr" {
  type      = "Microsoft.ContainerRegistry/registries@2023-01-01-preview"
  name      = "apressacr"
  parent_id = azurerm_resource_group.rg.id
  location  = azurerm_resource_group.rg.location

  body = jsonencode({
    sku = {
      name = "Standard"
    }
```

```
  properties = {
    adminUserEnabled = true
  }
})

tags = {
  "Key" = "DEV"
}

response_export_values = ["properties.loginServer", "properties.policies.
quarantinePolicy.status"]
}

output "login_server" {
  value = jsondecode(azapi_resource.acr.output).properties.loginServer
}
```

Managing Secrets in Azure Key Vault and Azure DevOps

In this section, we're going to explore how to retrieve Secrets from Azure Key Vault with Azure Pipeline. Azure Key Vault is an Azure cloud service that allows us to store and manage sensitive information like security keys, certificates, and credentials.

Azure Key Vault allows us to access sensitive information programmatically using tools like PowerShell, .NET, Python, and, in our case, Azure Pipelines. The advantage of Key Vault is that DevOps engineers don't need to use hard-to-code passwords and sensitive information for their code.

Note   You can skip the deployment section if you have an existing Key Vault store.

Deploying Azure Key Vault Using Terraform

In case you don't have Key Vault up and running, you can use the following code to deploy it to your subscription using Terraform.

Full Terraform Code

The end-to-end Terraform code is shown below.

```
terraform {
  required_providers {
    azurerm = {
      source = "hashicorp/azurerm"
    }
  }
}

provider "azurerm" {
  features {
    key_vault {
      purge_soft_delete_on_destroy = true
    }
  }
}

data "azurerm_client_config" "current" {}

resource "azurerm_resource_group" "rg" {
  name     = "apresstfchapter06"
  location = "australiaeast"
}

resource "azurerm_key_vault" "azvault" {
  name                        = "keyvault"
  location                    = azurerm_resource_group.rg.location
  resource_group_name         = azurerm_resource_group.rg.name
  enabled_for_disk_encryption = true
  tenant_id                   = data.azurerm_client_config.current.
                                tenant_id
  soft_delete_retention_days  = 7
  purge_protection_enabled    = false

  sku_name = "standard"
```

```
access_policy {
  tenant_id = data.azurerm_client_config.current.tenant_id
  object_id = data.azurerm_client_config.current.object_id

  key_permissions = [
    "get",
  ]

  secret_permissions = [
    "get",
  ]

  storage_permissions = [
    "get",
  ]
  }
}
```

Once you've deployed the code successfully, open the Azure portal.

Creating a Secret in Azure Key Vault

To create a Secret in Azure Key Vault, follow these steps:

1. Search the deployed Key Vault.

2. Under "Objects," click "Secrets," as shown in Figure 6-24.

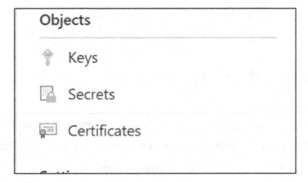

Figure 6-24. *Selecting "Secrets"*

3. Next, click "Generate/import," create a new Secret, and call it "Test."

Connecting Azure Key Vault to Azure Pipelines

Now it's time to connect and integrate our newly created Azure Key Vault to Azure Pipelines.

To do so:

1. Under "Pipelines" in the Azure DevOps project, click "Library," as shown in Figure 6-25.

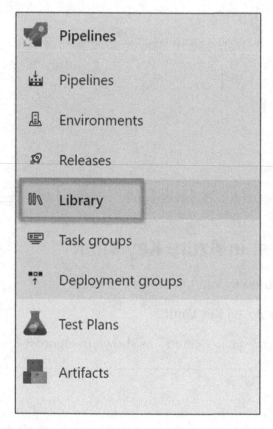

Figure 6-25. *Choosing "Library" in "Pipelines"*

2. When you get to the "Library" page, click the plus sign next to the "Variable group" button as shown to create a new group. This group will create a connection between the two services.

3. In the create new variable group details, fill in the group name; turn on "Link Secrets from an Azure Key vault as variables"; and select the name of the Azure Key Vault from the drop-down list and authorize it, as shown in Figure 6-26.

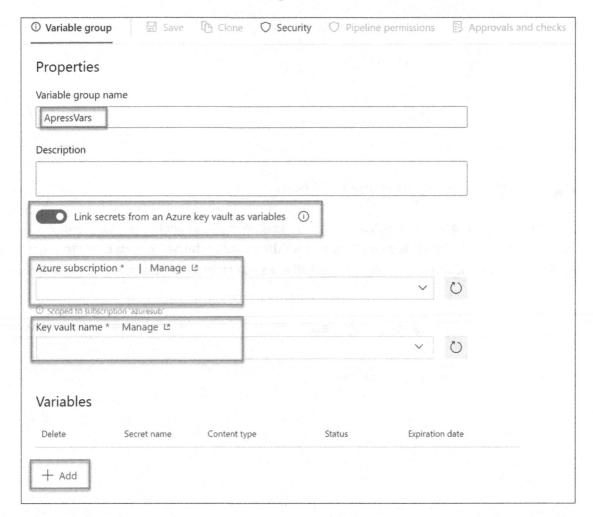

Figure 6-26. *"Variable group" screen*

Accessing Key Vault Secrets from a YAML Pipeline

To access Secrets stored in Azure Key Vault from a YAML pipeline, edit or create a new YAML pipeline. In the pipeline, search under "Tasks" for Azure Key Vault, as shown in Figure 6-27.

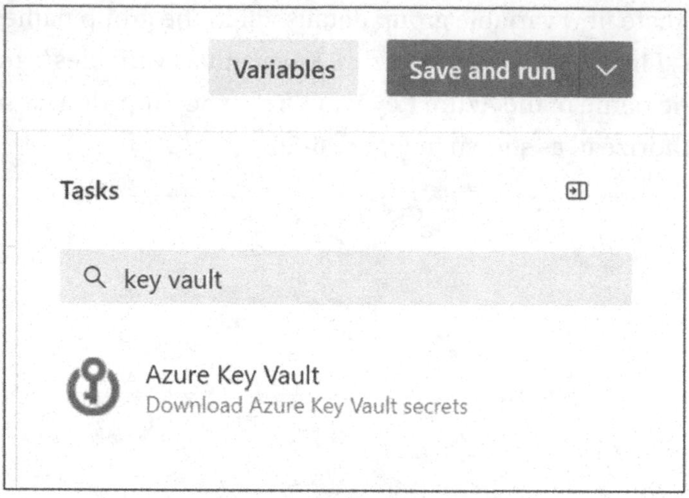

Figure 6-27. *Searching for Azure Key Vault*

For the details of Azure Key Vault, shown in Figure 6-28, select the names of your "Azure subscription" and "key vault" and enter the name of the Secret you'd like to retrieve. You can also use the * sign to load all the Secrets into the playbook.

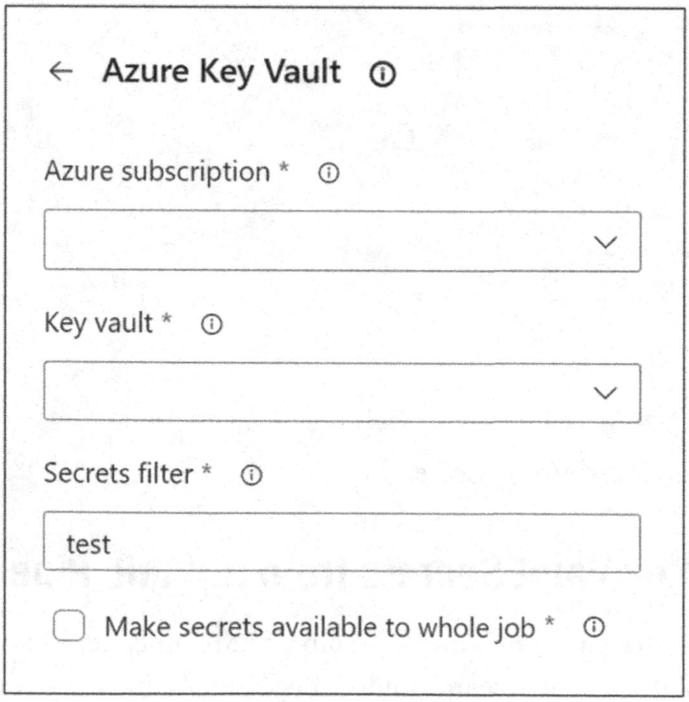

Figure 6-28. *Filling in the Azure Key Vault task details*

After you add the details, add the code to the pipeline. The code in the YAML file should look like this:

```
trigger:
- main

pool:
  vmImage: ubuntu-latest

steps:
- task: AzureKeyVault@2
  inputs:
    azureSubscription: 'AZURE SUBSCRIPTION'
    KeyVaultName: apress
    SecretsFilter: 'test'
    RunAsPreJob: true
```

Accessing Secrets from an Azure Pipeline

Once the task is added, every time the pipeline runs, the task will load the Secrets and make them available to tasks in the pipeline. To access a Secret stored in a pipeline, use the following two examples:

```
• task: CmdLine@2
  inputs:
   script: 'echo $(test)'

• powershell: |
      Write-Host "My secret variable is $env:MyVAR"
  env:
   MyVAR: $(test)
```

The first code block uses a simple command-line task. The second block uses the Microsoft PowerShell task. These examples show how sensitive information can be used in Azure Pipeline tasks.

A complete YAML pipeline will look like this:

```
trigger:
- main

pool:
  vmImage: ubuntu-latest

steps:
- task: AzureKeyVault@2
  inputs:
    azureSubscription: 'AZURE SUBSCRIPTION'
    KeyVaultName: 'vaultname'
    SecretsFilter: 'test'
    RunAsPreJob: true

- task: CmdLine@2
  inputs:
    script: 'echo $(test)'

- powershell: |
      Write-Host "My secret variable is $env:MyVAR"
  env:
    MyVAR: $(test)
```

Summary

In this chapter, we focused on the core services of Azure DevOps and the integration of Terraform and Azure using the platform. We also explored how to use Azure Repos and Azure Pipelines.

Additionally, we learned how to configure the Terraform extension for Azure DevOps, created an Azure Container Registry using an Azure pipeline, and used a remote state to save the deployment.

In the last two sections of the chapter, we built and pushed a Docker image to ACR using a pipeline and used the AzAPI to access the latest version of Azure REST API to deploy an ACR.

CHAPTER 7

Azure Compliance and Security

Introduction

In the last chapter of this book, I'd like to focus on a few security and compliance services that can help us keep our Azure environment safe and protected from malicious code and vulnerabilities.

In the last few years and since the release of the first edition of this book, Microsoft has invested a lot of resources in developing tools and services that can easily and seamlessly integrate with Azure services and even Azure DevOps.

This chapter will focus on going over how to use Microsoft Defender for Cloud to secure and stay compliant with our Azure workload, specifically Azure DevOps and container services.

Defender for Cloud

Defender for Cloud is Microsoft Azure's main cloud security and compliance service that offers protection against malicious code and vulnerabilities, using components that target specific Azure workloads. A sub service of Defender for Cloud is Defender for Containers which allow us to protect workloads running on AKS, ACR and other container related services.

For example, the Defender for Containers service allows users to protect Kubernetes nodes and clusters in real time. Defender for DevOps can be used to scan code, like that for Terraform configuration, against vulnerabilities in Docker images.

189

© Shimon Ifrah 2024
S. Ifrah, *Getting Started with Containers in Azure*, https://doi.org/10.1007/978-1-4842-9972-2_7

Defender for Container's full list of feature includes:

- protecting Kubernetes clusters running on AKS

- detecting misconfigurations in AKS

- vulnerability assessment for Docker images stored in ACR

- vulnerability assessment for images running in AKS

- runtime threat protection for nodes and clusters

- providing alerts about threats

- ensuring compliance of AKS clusters with industry best practices

Like most of the Azure cloud services, Defender for Cloud costs money. Figure 7-1 shows the price of each feature in Defender for Cloud's suite of services.

4 Defender CSPM Resources	$5	Billable resource/Month
2 Servers (Plan 2)	$15	Server/Month
0 App Service instances	$15	Instance/Month
0 Azure SQL Databases	$15	Server/Month
0 SQL servers on machines ⓘ	$15 $0.015	Server/Month Core/Hour
0 Open-source relational databases	$15	Server/Month
2 Storage accounts	$10 $0.15	Storage account/Month ⓘ GB scanned (Malware Scanning) ⓘ
0 Azure Cosmos DB accounts	$0.0012	100RU/s per hour
0 Containers ⓘ	$7	VM core/Month
2 Key Vaults	$0.25	Vault/Month
Resource Manager ⓘ	$5	Subscription/Month
0 Azure API Management services	Free(preview)	

Figure 7-1. *Price list for Defender for Cloud's suite of services*

Since this book is about Terraform, we'll deploy the Defender for Cloud's Defender for Containers service using Terraform.

Setting Up Azure with Defender for Containers

To get started, we'll enable Defender for Containers using Terraform. I've created the following Terraform configurations file, which is located in the repository of this book under Chapter 7.

Before you run the code, make sure to set your contact details in the `azurerm_security_center_contact`.

If you take a look at the code, you'll notice that we need to create a log analytics workspace.

Full Configuration Code

To deploy Microsoft Defender for Containers, run Terraform from the Chapter 7 located in the repository. Make sure you review the following plan output before deploying it to understand which services will be enabled and deployed:

```
data "azurerm_subscription" "current" {}

resource "azurerm_resource_group" "rg" {
  name     = "apresstfchapter07"
  location = "australiasoutheast"
}

resource "azurerm_log_analytics_workspace" "la_workspace" {
  name                = "apresstflog"
  location            = azurerm_resource_group.rg.location
  resource_group_name = azurerm_resource_group.rg.name
  sku                 = "PerGB2018"
  retention_in_days   = 30
}

resource "azurerm_security_center_workspace" "defender" {
  scope        = data.azurerm_subscription.current.id
  workspace_id = azurerm_log_analytics_workspace.la_workspace.id
}
```

```
resource "azurerm_security_center_subscription_pricing" "pricing" {
  tier          = "Standard"
  resource_type = "Containers"
}

resource "azurerm_security_center_contact" "contact" {
  name  = "Full Name"
  email = "Email"
  phone = "phone"
  alert_notifications = true
  alerts_to_admins    = true
}
resource "azurerm_security_center_auto_provisioning" "autoprovision" {
  auto_provision = "On"
}

resource "azurerm_subscription_policy_assignment" "va-auto-provisioning" {
  name                 = "mdc-autoprovisioning"
  display_name         = "Configure machines to receive a vulnerability
                          assessment provider"
  policy_definition_id = "/providers/Microsoft.Authorization/policyDefinitions/
                          13ce0167-8ca6-4048-8e6b-f996402e3c1b"
  subscription_id      = data.azurerm_subscription.current.id
  identity {
    type = "SystemAssigned"
  }
  location = "East US"
  parameters = <<PARAMS
{ "vaType": { "value": "mdeTvm" } }
PARAMS
}

resource "azurerm_role_assignment" "va-auto-provisioning-identity-role" {
  scope                = data.azurerm_subscription.current.id
  role_definition_id = "/providers/Microsoft.Authorization/roleDefinitions/
                        fb1c8493-542b-48eb-b624-b4c8fea62acd"
```

```
principal_id        = azurerm_subscription_policy_assignment.va-auto-
                       provisioning.identity[0].principal_id
}
```

Checking the Deployment

You can perform the following checks to ensure the code was deployed successfully:

1. To check if Microsoft Defender for Cloud was deployed
   successfully, open the Azure portal, and search for "Microsoft
   Defender for Cloud" as shown in Figure 7-2.

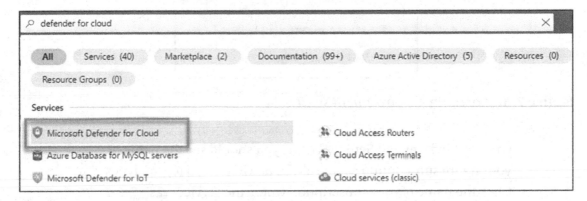

Figure 7-2. *Checking that the Defender for Cloud service has been successfully deployed*

2. To check if the service was enabled successfully, scroll down to the
   "Management" section on the Defender for Cloud main page and
   click "Environment settings," as shown in Figure 7-3.

Figure 7-3. *Locating "Environment settings"*

3. On the "Environment Settings" page, you should see the name of your Azure subscription as well as the newly created log analytics. Click the name of your subscription where the service was enabled.

4. In the list of services, make sure the status of the "Containers" plan is set to "On," as shown in Figure 7-4.

Plan	Pricing	Resource quantity	Monitoring coverage	Status
Servers	Plan 2 ($15/Server/Month) ⓘ Change plan >	1 servers		On ⬤Off
App Service	$15/Instance/Month ⓘ Details >	0 instances		On ⬤Off
Databases	Selected: 0/4 ⓘ Select types >	Protected: 0/0 instances		On ⬤Off
Storage	$10/Storage account/month On-upload malware scanning ($0.15/GB) ⓘ Details >	0 storage accounts		On ⬤Off
Containers	$7/VM core/Month ⓘ Details >	0 container registries; 0 kubernetes cores	⚠ Partial Settings >	⬤On Off
Key Vault	$0.25/Vault/Month Details >	1 key vaults		On ⬤Off
Resource Manager	$5/Subscription/Month ⓘ Details >			On ⬤Off
APIs	Free (preview) ⓘ Details >	0 Azure API Management services		On ⬤Off

∧ Cloud Workload Protection (CWP)

Microsoft Defender for Cloud provides comprehensive, cloud-native protections from development to runtime in multi-cloud environments.

Figure 7-4. *Defender plans*

5. Click the "Settings" button in the Containers plan line to enable additional services. To see the service in action, go ahead and deploy an AKS cluster from the Chapter 5 configuration files located in the repository of this book.

6. To check the status of container protection, click "Workload protections" on the Defender for Cloud main page and note the status of "Containers," as shown in Figure 7-5.

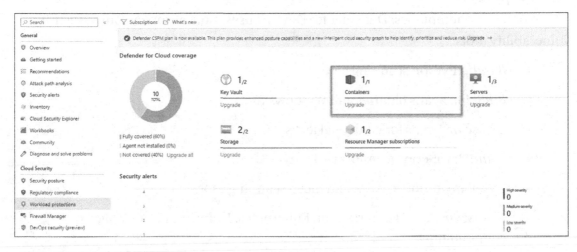

Figure 7-5. *Checking the status of container protection*

7. To view the status of the Container image scanning service, click the "Container image scanning" icon in the "Advanced Protection" section, as shown in Figure 7-6.

Figure 7-6. *Checking the status of container image scanning*

8. Once you click the icon, the number of vulnerabilities (if any) and unhealthy registries will be listed.

Securing IaC Code with Defender for DevOps

In this section, we'll learn how to use Microsoft Defender for Cloud DevOps Security, or Defender for DevOps, to protect source code and CI/CD pipelines across Azure Repos and GitHub.

Defender for DevOps works by connecting to a central repository service like Azure Repos and GitHub, scanning code for vulnerabilities, and checking if the code complies with best practices.

To detect vulnerabilities, Defender for DevOps uses multiple open-source security vulnerability tools:

- *Bandit*: Python scanning tool

- *BinSkim*: Scans binaries and Windows ELF

- *Credscan*: Scans for credential leaks

- *ESlint*: JavaScript scanning tool

- *Template Analyzer*: ARM and Bicep scanning tool

- *Terrascan*: Scans for Terraform, Kubernetes, Helm, and Dockerfile vulnerabilities

- *Trivy*: Scans for vulnerabilities in container images, file systems, and Git repositories

Installing Extensions

In Chapter 6, we learned about Azure DevOps extensions and installed the Terraform extension, which allowed us to use Terraform with Azure Pipelines. To scan for vulnerabilities and use Defender for DevOps, we need to install the following two extensions :

- Microsoft Security DevOps

- SARIF SAST Scans Tab (Static Analysis Results Interchange Format SAST Scans Tab)

The screen where you can download the Microsoft Security DevOps extension is shown in Figure 7-7.

Figure 7-7. *Downloading the Microsoft Security DevOps extension*

The screen where you can download the SARIF SAST Scans Tab extension is shown in Figure 7-8.

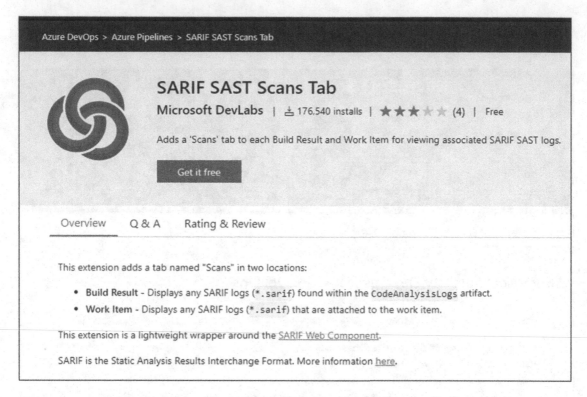

Figure 7-8. *Downloading the SARIF SAST Scans Tab extension*

Go ahead and install both extensions.

Connecting the Azure DevOps Organization to Defender for DevOps

Now that we've installed the extensions, it's time to connect our Azure DevOps organization to Defender for DevOps.

We can do that like this:

1. Open the Defender for Cloud main page.

2. Click "DevOps Security."

3. Click the "Add connector" button under "Connect DevOps environments," as shown in Figure 7-9.

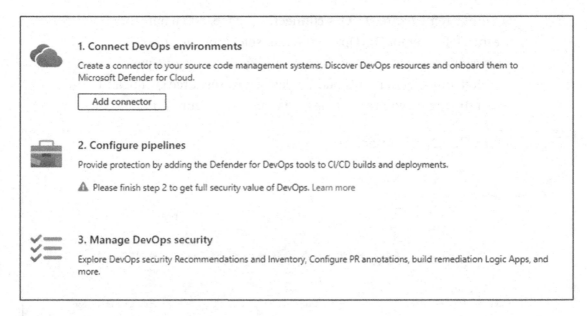

1. Connect DevOps environments

Create a connector to your source code management systems. Discover DevOps resources and onboard them to Microsoft Defender for Cloud.

Add connector

2. Configure pipelines

Provide protection by adding the Defender for DevOps tools to CI/CD builds and deployments.

⚠ Please finish step 2 to get full security value of DevOps. Learn more

3. Manage DevOps security

Explore DevOps security Recommendations and Inventory, Configure PR annotations, build remediation Logic Apps, and more.

Figure 7-9. *Adding the connector*

4.   On the "Environment settings" page, click "+ Add environment" and select "Azure DevOps (preview)," as shown in Figure 7-10.

Figure 7-10. *Adding the environment*

5. On the "Create Azure DevOps connection" page, add a name
    for the Defender for DevOps connector; select the type of
    subscription you want (it needs to be the same as the one you
    enabled for Defender for Cloud); create a new resource group; and
    select the region you're working in, as shown in Figure 7-11.

Create Azure DevOps connection ···
Azure DevOps connection | PREVIEW

① Connector details   ② Select plans   ③ Authorize connection   ④ Review and create

> ⚠ Warning - The Security Admin role assignment was not detected for the logged-in user, under the currently scoped subscription. This
> may lead to reduced functionality when interacting with connectors.

Enter a descriptive name for the Defender for DevOps instance, choose a Subscription and Resource Group to store the connection
information.

Name *	Select a name
Subscription * ⓘ	Pay-As-You-Go ⌄
└─ Resource group * ⓘ	⌄
	Create new
Region *	Australia East ⌄
	Defender for DevOps only supports Australia East, Central US and West Europe during preview

Figure 7-11. *The "Create Azure DevOps connection" page*

Enabling the Plan

Now, we need to enable the Containers plan. At this stage, the service is in preview and
doesn't cost anything.

   To activate the plan, let's take the following steps:

1. Go to the page where you select the plan located under Defender
    for Cloud, Environment Settings as shown in Figure 7-12.

Figure 7-12. *The "Select plans" page*

2. Next, we need to authorize Defender for DevOps to access the Azure DevOps resources, which is the most important step in the configuration. As shown in Figure 7-13, click the "Authorize" button and then go through the processes for authenticating and authorizing the connection between the two services. Make sure you click the "Accept" button when you're done.

Figure 7-13. *Authorizing the connection between Azure DevOps and Defender for Cloud*

3. In the "Edit connector account," we now need to select how we'd like to allow Defender for DevOps to discover projects. The first and recommended option is to authorize this to be done at the organization level, so that it autodiscovers all the projects in the DevOps organization. The second option allows us to limit the scope of authorization to specific projects. Figure 7-14 shows the project discovery options.

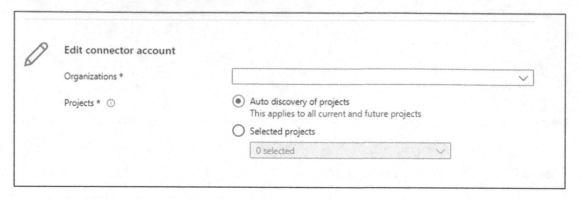

Figure 7-14. Options for discovery of projects

4. To complete the connection process, click "Create." Note that the discovery process will take around four hours to complete.

5. To check and review the status of the connection and see all the reviewed projects, go back to the DevOps Security page. You can access the page from the Defender for Cloud home page in the "Cloud Security" section. Figure 7-15 shows the DevOps Security page with the stats about the connector and the number of projects.

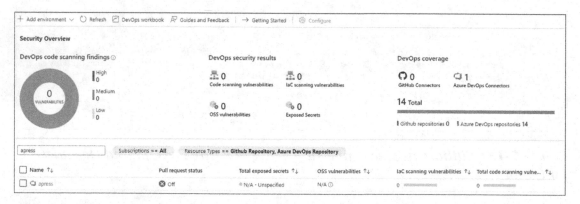

Figure 7-15. The DevOps "Security Overview" page

In the next exercise, we'll run a pipeline and integrate the IaC scanning tool to scan our code.

Scanning a Terraform Pipeline for Vulnerabilities

Now that Defender for DevOps is fully configured and connected to our DevOps organization, let's utilize the tool and see it in action. In this exercise, we'll use the DevOps Security extension in our pipeline to scan our Terraform code for vulnerabilities.

We can do that like this:

1. Log in to Azure DevOps and open the pipeline we created and let's add the following code block:

```
task: MicrosoftSecurityDevOps@1
displayName: 'Defender for DevOps Security Scan'
```

This task will scan the code using all the vulnerability tools available; however, if you'd like to limit the scope and only scan for IaC vulnerabilities, you can use the following task:

```
task: MicrosoftSecurityDevOps@1
  inputs:
    categories: 'IaC'
```

The full code should look like this:

```
trigger:
- none

pool:
  vmImage: ubuntu-latest

steps:
- task: TerraformInstaller@0
  inputs:
    terraformVersion: 'latest'

- task: MicrosoftSecurityDevOps@1
  displayName: 'Defender for DevOps Security Scan'

- task: TerraformTaskV3@3
  inputs:
    provider: 'azurerm'
    command: 'init'
```

```
      workingDirectory: '$(System.DefaultWorkingDirectory)/
      chapter06/Create_ACR'
      backendServiceArm: 'AZURE SUBSCRIPTION'
      backendAzureRmResourceGroupName: 'tfstate'
      backendAzureRmStorageAccountName: 'tfstates14w8'
      backendAzureRmContainerName: 'tfstate'
      backendAzureRmKey: 'Create_acr.terraform.tfstate'

  - task: TerraformTaskV3@3
    inputs:
      provider: 'azurerm'
      command: 'plan'
      workingDirectory: '$(System.DefaultWorkingDirectory)/
      chapter06/Create_ACR'
      environmentServiceNameAzureRM: 'AZURE SUBSCRIPTION'

  - task: TerraformTaskV3@3
    inputs:
      provider: 'azurerm'
      command: 'apply'
      workingDirectory: '$(System.DefaultWorkingDirectory)/
      chapter06/Create_ACR'
      environmentServiceNameAzureRM: 'AZURE SUBSCRIPTION '
```

2. You can add the extra code from the Azure pipeline directly or
    using VS Code and push the changes. Run the pipeline check and
    wait for it to complete. Once finished, click the "Scans" tab on the
    job summary page, as shown in Figure 7-16.

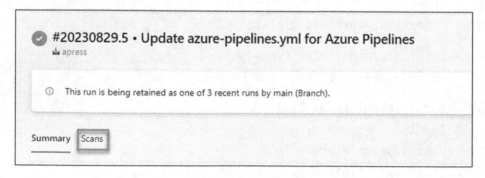

Figure 7-16. *"Scans" tab on the job summary page*

3. The "Scans" tab will list all the vulnerabilities and best practice recommendations that showed up in the scan. Figure 7-17 shows some of the recommendations that might be made as a result of the scan.

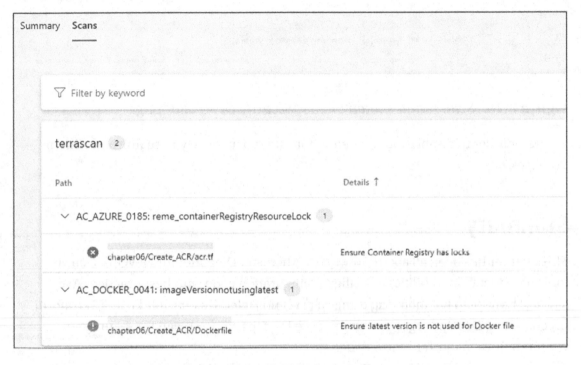

Figure 7-17. Recommendations based on scan results

4. Now, let's go back to the "Security Overview" page in the Defender for DevOps console, as shown in Figure 7-18, and check the results of the scan. Once the scan is completed, results and stats will sync almost immediately to Defender for DevOps.

In our case, the scan found three vulnerabilities that should be addressed, as shown in the figure.

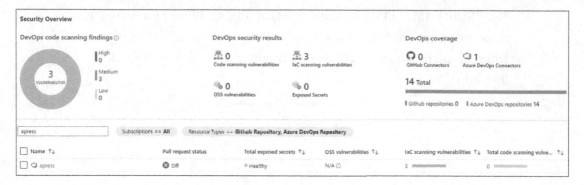

Figure 7-18. *Scan results shown on the "Security Overview" page*

Remember to disable your Defender for Cloud plan once you're finished with the exercises.

Summary

This chapter has been all about how to use Microsoft Defender for DevOps security tools to detect vulnerabilities and align configuration code with best practices. We learned how to do the following things: (1) set up Defender for Cloud using Terraform; (2) connect a DevOps organization to Azure DevOps; and (3) scan for security vulnerabilities in the Terraform code.

Index

A

© Shimon Ifrah 2024
S. Ifrah, *Getting Started with Containers in Azure*, https://doi.org/10.1007/978-1-4842-9972-2

Printed in the United States
by Baker & Taylor Publisher Services